THE **TESTING** SERIES

HOW TO PASS
ASSESSMENT
CENTRES

BY KAREN MANNERING

THE **TESTING** SERIES
expert advice on test preparation

Orders: Please contact How2become Ltd, Suite 2, 50 Churchill Square Business Centre, Kings Hill, Kent ME19 4YU.

Telephone: (44) 0845 643 1299 – Lines are open Monday to Friday 9am until 5pm. Fax: (44) 01732 525965. You can also order via the e-mail address info@how2become.co.uk.

ISBN: 9781907558283

First published 2013

Typeset for How2become Ltd by Molly Hill, Canada.

Printed in Great Britain for How2become Ltd by CMP (uk) Limited, Dorset.

CONTENTS

WELCOME

Dear Sir/Madam

Welcome to Assessment Centres: your new definitive guide on how to perform well in job assessment centres. This guide has been designed to help you prepare for and pass any type of assessment centre. The author of this guide, Karen Mannering, is a fellow of the Chartered Institute of Personnel and Development and a member of both the Chartered Management Institute and the British Psychological Society. She has helped literally hundreds of people to get jobs through the assessment centre route together with designing assessment centres for clients and being an assessor and observer. You will find Karen's advice and techniques invaluable to your success in performing well throughout the assessment exercises.

Assessment centres can be a very nerve-wracking experience. The best way to counter this is to embark on a period of intensive preparation in the build up to the centre itself. The majority of employers will be assessing you against a set of competencies to look for certain behaviours, therefore it is always worth looking on the company's website to locate these and be familiar with them throughout this book.

If you would like any further assistance with your preparation for any kind of job interview, assessment centre or selection process, then we offer a wide range of products and training courses at the website:

WWW.HOW2BECOME.COM

Finally, you won't achieve much in life without hard work, determination and perseverance. Work hard, stay focused and be what you want!

Good luck and best wishes.

The how2become team

PREFACE
BY KAREN
MANNERING

Being told that you need to attend an assessment centre is sure to send most people running in the opposite direction. Hands up anyone who enjoys these things – well I don't suppose there would be many people with their hands up because the whole assessment centre concept can seem as though you are being judged, and how scary is that? This book is not only about how to ensure that you perform well in assessment centres, it is also aimed at helping you to change your mindset through explaining what assessment centres are, how they work, and what they are there to achieve. My belief is that when you understand them and how they are constructed, you begin to lose your fear of the process. They become familiar and you can instantly see what each activity is designed to test, leaving you free to perform to that end. You will feel so much more confident being measured if you know what you are a being measured against.

During my career I have interviewed many people and been involved with:

- coaching people for assessment centre success
- developing assessment centres
- running assessment centres, and
- being an assessor or observer.

I have seen people rise and excel in an assessment centre, and also totally fall apart. Unfortunately there is often no opportunity to do it again and therefore how you perform on the day is critical. Are some people good at assessment centres and others less competent? No – the difference is in how you prepared in the time leading up to the assessment centre –

and critical to that is how you prepare mentally. I will show you all the techniques I go through with the students I coach. At present I have a 95% success rate in securing people jobs through their attending assessment centres, but I can't run around the country coaching everyone, and for that reason, I decided to put all my thoughts into this book.

After my initial explanations as to how assessment centres work we will be looking together at specific aspects of the centre. To help us do this I have created a fictitious company, BabyMaxPro and you can see their case study towards the back of this book. Read this and be familiar with the company because we will be using this company as an illustration throughout the entire book. It is typical of the type of pre-reading you may receive as part of your preparation for an assessment centre. From there we will be looking at each aspect of the assessment centre in detail and working out what it means in real terms, and how you can impress. Simply understanding the background will imbue you with more confidence and free you up to concentrate on your performance.

While we are discussing your performance, it is vital that you work on your confidence. Assessment centres are run at a significant cost and therefore tend to be used either for high graded jobs or when the post is vital to the running of the business (jobs that are often referred to as 'key roles'). In other words there is a huge investment in selecting exactly the right person for the role. It is not enough to simply perform to a script. You need to have total confidence in yourself that you are indeed the right person for the job so that you not only tick the boxes, but you also come across as a strong and capable individual. Self-belief is essential to your success – no one is going to offer the job to someone who appears to perform well in tests but otherwise seems unsure. That is why we are also going to cover confidence and how you can achieve the right mindset. By the time you have finished reading this guide and worked on the assignments you will not only understand fully what is expected of you in each of the examples but you will also feel more confident in your approach to assessment centres.

Having coached so many people to success I strongly believe that great preparation, insight and planning can win the day. Take time to read and study this guide and you will find that you not only perform consistently well in assessment centres but that you positively relish them!

Best wishes
Karen Mannering

CHAPTER 1
HERE'S THE THING

Let's start by making an assumption. You are probably reading this book because you have either been asked to attend an assessment centre or need to know more about the whole process. Perhaps it is for a new job, a promotion, or maybe you are being assessed for a restructure in your organisation. You may have some knowledge about assessment centres, or maybe you are starting right from the beginning. One thing is clear, you want to excel at the assessment centre and be offered that role.

This book is designed to provide everything you need to know so that you feel comfortable on the day and recognise each activity for what it is trying to achieve. You will know what the organisation is measuring and how to perform in a way that not only matches their requirements but exceeds them. By taking a measured and calm approach to the assessment centre, you will be ready for any activity they may present to you. You will not be surprised or shocked, you will be expecting each activity and instead of entering panic mode (and losing valuable minutes while you worry even further about your scrambled brain) you will hit the ground running and be ready to focus in on the crux of the activity, and gain those valuable points.

In my career I have coached many people through assessment centres and I feel it is important to cover some fundamental questions before we look at the elements that make up a typical assessment centre. There are a number of popular questions that people ask me and I have laid those out in this chapter, with a comprehensive answer for each.

Following this overview in chapter 1, and a chapter on gaining a motivational mindset, the remaining chapters in this book (3-9) take you through the elements of a typical assessment centre, and deal with each individually. At the very end of the book there is one case study – BabyMaxPro. I have created this case study to provide a fictitious organisation that we can use throughout the entire book to assess how an organisation will form its assessment activities and exercises. This will help you to think through your responses with me, and check some of your answers against my thoughts.

Note: in a real assessment centre the organisers may use as a background to the tasks:

- your own organisation (if it is a reorganisation and therefore you know the background history)

- their organisation (if you are going for a job in a new organisation it is unlikely you have great in depth information about their organisation)

- a fictitious case study such as the BabyMaxPro example (if they want everyone to know and use only the same information).

WHAT IS AN ASSESSMENT CENTRE?

An assessment centre is a number of activities that are arranged together to test your responses. They are typically based on competencies or behaviours that the organisation who holds the job, feel are important for their staff to have, together with requiring you to demonstrate certain skills.

Some of the activities are tested over one or two days (usually in one venue), whilst others may be computer based tests that you access via the internet, either before or after the assessment centre itself.

The most important aspect of an assessment centre is that it tests and measures your performance against the skills, knowledge and abilities required for the job. For example, there would be no point in me asking you to "Please enter the room opposite where you will find an elephant and pair of pyjamas. I want you to get the pyjamas on the elephant" – if fitting large and unusual objects into tight, unforgiving clothing were not part of that job.

Important note – assessment centres are there to measure performance in a role that is similar to one required in the actual job.

WHAT SHOULD I EXPECT?

Assessment centres can be run at any level and for any length of time. However, their complexity and format should replicate the job. For example an assessment centre for a senior manager or director may be held over two days, whereas an assessment centre for a more junior member of staff may be one afternoon.

When you arrive at an assessment centre full details of the programme will be given to you and you will be aided by helpers to take part in a number of activities. These may be in different rooms, with varying observers. For some activities you may be on your own and for others you may be with other applicants. For some activities you may need to collaborate and in others you may be adversaries.

In this book I will be covering the range of typical activities, namely:

- psychometrics
- in-tray exercises
- group activities
- presentations
- workplace report
- interviews (personal and media).

These are all individual types of activities and they are woven together to form an assessment centre. Depending on the job you apply for, you could be asked to undertake one or all of these. There may also be multiple tests of the same activity (such as two different group activities or varying psychometric tests). Also there may be combinations of activities to test certain skills, for example, when testing your level of decisiveness this could include the results from your psychometrics, a group activity AND the interview.

As mentioned above all activities are designed to test critical aspects of the job, and in most cases your behaviour will be numerically rated against competencies.

WHAT ARE COMPETENCIES AND HOW ARE THEY USED?

Let me take you back into the dim and distant past, a past where computers were new technology and good organisational skills could take you a long way. If you were looking for a capable administration officer it was easy to select staff because an employer only had to put in the advertisement 'Must be able to use a computer and type at 30 words per minute' and already the number of people applying for the job more than halved. In a way it was a great selection tool because it meant that any employer could whittle down their application list even further by asking the applicants to take a computer typing test on the day of the interview. Would that put you off? Well it would if you were unsure about computers and typing. Another similar request could be 'Must be able to type at 30 words per minute.' Now that is actually not very fast typing, and I am sure that everyone reading this book could actually type at faster than that already, but back then, a simple measure like this was sufficient to short-list effectively, and narrow down the number of applicants to a more reasonable half dozen.

So why are we not using these measures today? Well, I gave you a hint in the last sentence above. Such is the amount of technology in our homes and schools, the gadgets that we use, and quality of training programmes, these no longer become good measures for selection. The truth is that most people today applying for an office job can type at 30 words per minute or more, use a computer proficiently, and if that is the case, then we need to look at different measures for streamlining our selection.

The answer to this conundrum came in the form of competencies, and the logic to using them is fairly simple – we are able to train you to use a computer, use all manner of software, maintain files and databases, but (and here is the BIG BUT) we cannot train you to have the right attitude, ethos, and values that fit our organisation, and these manifest themselves in the behaviour we want you to exhibit.

Let's just be clear about this – assessment centres aim to measure our observed behaviour in addition to any skills or qualifications we may hold.

Recruiting a new manager is very expensive, typically around £3,000 – £5,000 from advertisement through to the end of their induction. It is a very expensive mistake to employ a candidate that does not fit into the organisation or wish to honour its values. One careless member of staff can do irreparable damage to a company and therefore all organisations need to know that their managers exhibit the right set of behaviours that dovetail with the way their business operates. But how do we test and measure those attitudes, values and ethos? This is where competencies come into their own.

Competencies are simply statements of behaviour that the organisation is expecting. Some of these behaviours could be around dealing with other people and others could be practical. For example, competencies for a project manager could include:

- Be able to motivate and influence others
- Identifies priorities
- Identifies key areas of risk
- Allocates resources appropriately
- Manages their own and other's time
- Has a 'can-do' approach.

I hope you will agree that these are just some of the areas that would be typically considered necessary for a project manager to have and therefore any organisation would want to test their candidates against. They are crucial for the job of Project Manager and the final one is essential for BabyMaxPro as it has set its sights on international growth which it hopes to achieve through high levels of customer care.

EXERCISE

I have reproduced this list on the next page. Imagine that you have been given the job of testing out these applicants against this list. What activities could you ask them to do that would test each of these very simple competencies?

COMPETENCIES:

BE ABLE TO MOTIVATE AND INFLUENCE OTHERS

IDENTIFIES PRIORITIES

IDENTIFIES KEY AREAS OF RISK

ALLOCATES RESOURCES APPROPRIATELY

MANAGES THEIR OWN AND OTHER'S TIME

HAS A 'CAN-DO' APPROACH

How did you do? There are no strict right or wrong ideas but here are some of my notes.

COMPETENCIES

BE ABLE TO MOTIVATE AND INFLUENCE OTHERS

I could ask the candidates to simulate a negotiation where they have to influence other people to accept a compromise agreement.

I could ask the candidate to speak to someone who has poor performance and low motivation issues in the hope of gaining an agreement from them to try to improve in the future.

IDENTIFIES PRIORITIES

I could give the candidates a list of tasks and ask them to prioritise them.

I could give the candidates a Gant chart of a project that has gone wrong and ask them to identify what actions they need to take to redeem the situation, and in which priority order.

IDENTIFIES KEY AREAS OF RISK

I could give the candidates a project plan and ask them to write a report on where the areas of risk lay and how they would create a contingency plan.

I would show the candidates the project plan and also a risk report from a consultant that has identified some key areas of concern. I would then ask them to write a report to comment on these areas and state what actions they would take.

ALLOCATES RESOURCES APPROPRIATELY

Using the same project plan I could ask them to either write a report concerning the resource allocation, undertake a costing exercise, or find 'hidden' mistakes.

Ask the candidate to present (and justify) to the Board the need for more resources.

MANAGES THEIR OWN AND OTHER'S TIME

I could simulate a situation where the candidates are put under pressure and the actual activity is impossible to complete in the time available. They will be forced to manage their time appropriately.

I could introduce a role play whereby someone 'plays' a member of staff who is having trouble with their time management, and needs help.

HAS A 'CAN-DO' APPROACH

Throughout the other exercises I can look at how proactive the candidates are in their suggestions. Do they appear keen to find solutions and move projects forward? Are they flexible in their approach?

Competencies exist to measure your behaviour in real work situations, and they will be tested through activities at the assessment centre.

Some of the competencies will have one main activity set against them, others (such as the final one shown – **Has a 'can-do' approach**) lie across all the activities and therefore would be assessed throughout.

Important point!

If you have been asked to attend an assessment centre, the organisation should enclose a list of their competencies with your instructions. If you don't have this, then either ring their personnel department and ask for a set of their organisational competencies or search on their website. You need to know what you are going to be measured against, so that you can prepare effectively.

Now let's look at some of those questions that I am often asked.

WHY HAVE I BEEN ASKED TO ATTEND AN ASSESSMENT CENTRE?

By now you know that holding an assessment centre can be quite an expensive business. There can be:

- The cost of the centre (hiring of rooms and refreshments)

- The cost of the observers and/or interviewers (these could be other members of staff, paid consultants or occupational psychologists)

- The cost of the materials, psychometric tests, and exercises (if they have been bought in)

- Candidate expenses (some organisations will reimburse the candidate's expenses for attending the assessment centre).

Altogether this represents a significant investment by the organisation to finding exactly the right person for the post. Therefore assessment centres are not run for every post, only the ones where the investment is justified.

Quite simply if you have been asked to attend an assessment centre, rather than feeling nervous you should pat yourself on the back. It means that this role is considered so significant that getting it wrong is not an option, hence the level of investment and your involvement.

HOW WILL THEY MARK AND MEASURE ME?

When you undertook the exercise in suggesting ways to measure competencies earlier I am sure that you came up with a number of different methods for testing. For example, one might be writing an essay and another may be undertaking an activity whilst being observed. Therefore the essay would be marked after the event by one marker (to enable consistency) and the observed activity would be observed by several 'observers' who mark the behaviour they see on a chart like the one on the following page.

The first example shows a free-text form that would be used by an observer watching two applicants. As a rule of thumb, the observer sitting opposite you is your main observer, but to help with fairness and consistency most observers will watch two applicants at a time. **A** is their main observation, but they will also keep an eye on **B**. On the sheet they will record the time that **A** does something (this make it easier to track back later), what **A** actually does, and their comment. Following the form I have also produced an example of a completed one for you to see. The results of the two observers are compared later.

The second example shows you a typical rating sheet for an exercise whereby the applicant is being assessed against specific competences. This is not free-text in that the observer is not there to look for any generally interesting behaviour but is there to capture evidence only about specific points that relate to the competencies, and then give them a rating. Once again I have provided a completed example one for you to see.

At the end of the full assessment centre, all the marks and comments are collated and the observers will have a meeting with the employer to discuss the results.

EXAMPLE 1

An example of a form that could be used for behavioural observation of two applicants

Assessor: . . . .

Person A: . . . . Person B: . . . .

Date: . . . . Venue: . . . .

Time	Record of person A	Observers comments	Record of person B

An example of a form that could be used for behavioural observation of two applicants

Assessor: *Melanie Strong*

Person A: *Susan Carter*   Person B: *William Black*

Date: *11 May 20***   Venue: *Lymington House Conference Centre*

Time	Record of person A	Observers comments	Record of person B
9.31	Introduced themselves	Highly assertively	Introduced themselves
9.33		Short intro, no additional details	
10.05	Took up the flip chart pen to make graphic notes and diagrams for the group	An assertive action that was not challenged by the group	Appeared to passively accept the action
10.34		Challenged the assumptions made by the group. Looked anxious and tried to get others on his side	Sat forward and began to truly engage

EXAMPLE 2

A typical rating sheet against competencies

Competencies	Positive evidence	Negative evidence	Rating (1-5)
Be able to motivate and influence others			
Identifies priorities			
Identifies key areas of risk			
Allocates resources appropriately			
Manages their own and other's time			
Has a 'can-do' approach.			

Showed multiple clear evidence of competence with examples and no substantial negative evidence	5
Showed clear evidence of competence with some examples and very little negative evidence	4
On balance showed more positive evidence than negative evidence	3
Showed sufficient negative evidence to be considered lacking in competence	2
Showed either multiple clear evidence of lack of competence or no evidence at all	1

Part of the sheet completed

Competencies	Positive evidence	Negative evidence	Rating (1-5)
Be able to motivate and influence others	Gave two examples of how he had motivated others to succeed	Gave one example of a failure to motivate	3
Identifies priorities	Clear evidence of working to deadlines and prioritising workload		5
Identifies key areas of risk	Demonstrated areas where he had used a risk plan to great effect		5
Allocates resources appropriately	Gave an example of his current project that is on budget	Admitted to a project that ran out of money	2
Manages their own and other's time	Worked very closely with a member of staff to help them meet deadlines		4
Has a 'can-do' approach.	Gave example of when he has 'gone the extra mile' at work		5

WEIGHTING

Weighting an assessment centre simply means that some factors may be more important than others. Using our earlier example of the competencies for a project manager, the employer may have said that greater emphasis should be placed on 'Has a can-do approach' than on any of the other competencies. If this is the case then it may be decided that the mark for that competency is doubled or considered first before any of the others.

You cannot find out in advance whether the scores will be weighted or not but if you read a line such as, 'Greater consideration will be given to those with exemplary attendance records' or 'Greater consideration will be given to those with superior communication skills' in any official documentation you receive as part of the assessment centre process, then it is likely that these factors will be weighted more highly. Unfortunately, even if you see this you will not know the degree of weighting, as competencies may be weighted in several ways such as:

- the scores for that section are doubled

- the scores for that section are increased by 50%

- the percentage for that section may be worth 50% of the whole score

Therefore, it is best not to worry about the amount of weighting and concentrate simply on the fact that **any** highlighted skill will be hotly observed and critically marked.

HOW WILL THEY USE THE RESULTS?

At the end of an assessment centre the marks will be added together and then typically a meeting will be held with all observers and the employing manager. Together they will discuss the outcome of each individual in detail and also discuss the exercises, how they were interpreted and whether there were any problems. In some instances feedback or management reports may be written which will draw all the outcomes of the tests together and present them in a cohesive document that can be used for future reference and learning.

As this is an intense (and expensive) process the employer will be expecting to find someone to appoint into the job from the assessment centre, and therefore it is important that the position is awarded on observed behaviours, knowledge and skill – otherwise there was no reason to run the assessment centre. This means that the final appointment should be based on the outcome of the assessment centre as a whole. However, because you have entered into all the tests whether you are offered the job or not you should receive some really useful feedback on your performance and may even be given a copy of your report.

WHAT IS THE DIFFERENCE BETWEEN AN ASSESSMENT CENTRE AND A DEVELOPMENT CENTRE?

In essence very little in composition or nature of the activities. However the purpose of an assessment centre is to assess someone against the competencies required for the job, whereas the purpose of a development centre is to place the candidate in a situation where they are working with the competences to see where their development needs are for the future. Development centres can be less stressful as your job is not on the line, and also more supportive in their tone and marking. As an applicant you know when you are entering an assessment centre that you are in competition with the other candidates as there is usually only one job. In a development centre you are not necessarily in competition with anyone else. You are trying out your skills in set scenarios and expect to find that you need additional development in some of those skills areas in your feedback.

INTRODUCTION TO THE CASE STUDY

Earlier in the chapter I mentioned that an assessment centre may use:

- your own organisation (if it is a reorganisation)
- their organisation (if you are going for a job in a new organisation)
- a fictitious case study (if they want everyone to know only the same information)

Let's just briefly look at the pros and cons of each approach.

Background to the assessment centre	Pros	Cons
Using your own organisation as a background case study	Examples can be grounded in reality eg. they can use the real organisational charts and a real situation The applicants will already feel comfortable with the data	Candidates have more emotional investment in the organisation and their responses could be about personalities rather than the job Not every organisation wishes to expose its problems (even for a case study) to candidates (some of whom may be from a rival company)
Using their organisation as a background case study even if you do not know that organisation	The examples are real and will give the candidates a 'feel' for working there As part of the assessment centre the employer can find out how much the potential employee really knows about the company (or whether they have done any research)	It is difficult to give the right amount of information to the candidates so that they can use it in a meaningful activity that enables them to create a viable response (you need to know enough information to make a logical decision) If you have internal and external candidates. This process can favour the internal candidate because they know more about the organisation
Using a fictitious case study	Every applicant reads the same information Everyone works with the same information and so any variance is down to knowledge or experience	It can be difficult to provide depth in a fictitious case study (eg you don't get a sense of culture or who the other players are) People generally loathe role play and may respond falsely (as if acting)

As you can see there are pros and cons for each approach. In writing this book I am assuming that my readers will be from many different organisations, and therefore, for illustration and guidance to possible responses I have included a case study (featured at the end of the book). This case study is totally fictitious and any resemblance to any current or previous business is purely circumstantial.

PLEASE READ THE CASE STUDY PAPERWORK ABOUT BABYMAXPRO NOW – you will find it at the very back of this book.

Feel free to make notes if you need to capture your initial thoughts.

Important points from this chapter:

1. Assessment centres are huge investments and need to be taken seriously.

2. Assessment centres are a number of activities grouped together to assess how you perform in particular situations.

3. Candidates are generally assessed against competencies so that their behaviour is observed.

4. There will be a background 'story' or case study that will be used to set the scene, and this could be real or fictitious.

5. You need to be very familiar with any case study and make notes on every aspect you find interesting or stands out for you.

6. Development centres are very similar in content to assessment centres but differ in their function.

7. There is much you can do to prepare for assessment centre success.

So, let's get going!

CHAPTER 2
CREATING THE RIGHT MINDSET

From reading the first chapter you may now be thinking, well if I am going to be tested on the spot, there is very little I can do about that, after all I won't know the questions before I go into the room. If you were thinking this, then I have to tell you that this is not exactly correct. There is plenty of preparation you can do for each of the activities but we need to start with your own mindset.

Henry Ford was attributed with once saying, 'Whether you think you can, or whether you think you can't – you're right.' It is a sobering thought that your mindset could ultimately decide the outcome of your performance at the assessment centre. Need convincing? Athletes don't enter a race thinking that it would be quite nice to win – they feel the power of winning surging through their veins. They prepare like crazy and know that they only have one shot at this and they focus on attaining their goal. Do you think like this? If you do, then great, you need to take this feeling into your work situation. However if you don't feel like this, we have some work to do, my friend, because you need to feel like a winner to be able to win.

YOUR MOST POWERFUL ORGAN

Your brain is the most powerful organ in your body. Close your eyes and concentrate and you can be anywhere you want to be, experiencing any manner of sensations – without even leaving your chair. Do we use this phenomenal power house to its full potential? I expect that you know that I am going to say no.

Of course you use your brain extensively in many everyday situations. When you drive a vehicle or navigate your way across a town you use tremendous brain power and when you feel taxed by a busy day, you may feel mentally tired out. This is your logical brain function being used to its full potential. It can sort out puzzles and solve problems galore, and you use it all the time to help you get through life. However, you also need to exercise the more creative function in your brain. This function taps into our senses and allows us to imagine other words, visualise colour and hear music – even when none is playing.

Let's do a quick experiment. Close your eyes and imagine a bar of chocolate (or any other sweet you prefer). See it in your head, feel it in your hands, sniff it and smell that wonderful sweetness. Now imagine taking a bite. What does it taste like? Is it velvety smooth in texture? Do the flavours tickle and run down your throat? Can you really imagine being in that moment? Sorry to break the illusion, but its time to open your eyes.

Hopefully that exercise convinced you that you can experience being in the moment using the creative function of your brain. For some people the creative brain function is not exercised as regularly as the logical function. If this is you do not fear because this exercise demonstrated that we all have the capacity to imagine sensations and feelings that seem very real. We are now going to take these creative feelings and make them work for us.

Tip: Do you remember the last time you had a bad dream? The feelings seemed so real but they only lasted until your logical brain took over and enabled you to 'forget' the dream. Once the memory has been wiped out, the fear is dissipated with it, but boy was that a scary one at the time! Some dreams we might want to forget but others we may want to stay with us. How fantastic it would be to be able to conjure up a happy moment, fantastic scene or even a feeling of complete and utter confidence. Imagine how brilliant it would be if you could not only have such vivid positive dreams, making you feel confident and ready for anything BUT ALSO be able to hang onto those feelings and take them into your working life! You could take on the world! -and that is just what you are going to do courtesy of zone thinking.

ZONE THINKING

Welcome to the zone! Ever wondered why sometimes you feel like you can move mountains, and on other days you want to crawl back under the duvet? It all depends on which zone you are in.

Your zone helps you to experience the world in different ways. For example if you think the world is dishing out some very bad vibes for you right now, you may be forgiven for slipping into in a very negative zone. Well, your mind is your own and you may have a very good reason for feeling this way, only the problem with this is that you start to view all situations through this zone filter and it begins to affect the whole of your life. You start to see everything through a negative veil, for example one outcome may be that you fail to recognise any opportunity that comes your way, perhaps because it seems 'too good to be true.' Oh dear, is there no way out?

Quick exercise: imagine that you have just come into work and seen a letter on your desk. You open it and it congratulates you on your efforts over the past year and offers you a 10% bonus, paid immediately. Don't you feel good? I'll bet you are feeling a foot taller already! Now imagine that half an hour has passed and your colleague walks in. They snatch up and open what looks like an identical letter from their desk and announce in a loud voice, 'Did everyone get one of these? 20%! I don't believe it!' Now how do you feel? Not quite as happy as before? Undervalued? You may start questioning your own performance or why this other person was awarded more. In other words, even though you have a 10% bonus you feel somewhat dissatisfied. Finally imagine that your manager rushes up to you and tells you that your letter has a typo, it is indeed 20% – how happy are you now?

The reason I asked you to undertake this activity is to show you how our positive and negative feelings can go up and down, triggered by feelings and events. And notice how the initial negative feelings triggered further negative thoughts, and the positive feelings promulgated further positive thoughts. To get a grip on this is to master our own thought patterns – and this is what you can easily achieve.

The truth is that when we think positively we are more open to ideas, we feel better and we are actually healthier – but how do you become more positive when you have slipped into negativity (such as in the example above?) To relieve you from this negative zone something has to change –

and that something has to be you. OK, in this example the trigger was reward but in the real world we cannot rely on anyone providing regular reward to enable us to feel good. Do we need someone to help us then? Regrettably no one can move you into another zone – only you can do it. In the example above you experienced briefly the difference that being in a more positive zone can bring. If you were able to trigger that at will you will not only want to use it more often, but you would also want to switch zones to suit different situations. Want to deal with a difficult staff issue? Enter a more empathic zone. Need to give a presentation? Then you need to trigger a strong and confident zone.

The ability to enter different zones is in all of us, but rather than choosing zones at random, we want zone thinking to work for us. If you are not used to thinking positively and feeling self confident, you may find that you need to practice a few times before you can begin to trust zone thinking to help you. In fact you may not even know what this zone feels like right now, but start to practice and you soon will.

EXERCISE

TRY THIS

Close your eyes and think about a time when you felt super confident. It does not matter what age you were, who you were with or what the situation was – the important fact is that you feel so confident that you could burst and can recall the feeling in detail, and 'see' the occasion in your mind.

Allow yourself to wallow in that feeling for a while. Don't worry if you find yourself smiling, no one can read your thoughts or whatever is being replayed in your head. This is the feeling that you need to recreate. Just experience it for a moment and enjoy!

OK, now you know what that zone feels like and how dynamic it makes you feel I'm sure you would like to be able to switch into that feeling at will. Imagine how wonderful it would be to be able to recreate that feeling every time you feel the need for a confidence boost – such as during the assessment centre. How fantastic would that be? – the truth is that you can, with a little practice!

TO CREATE ZONAL RECALL AT WILL

1. Find a quiet spot where you will not be disturbed for around ten minutes.

2. Close your eyes and take in three deep breaths in, and as you breathe out, feel the tension slipping from your body and ensure your shoulders are relaxed. Each breath should make you feel more relaxed and you may feel your body slump a little as your shoulders relax down.

3. Recall the situation again in your mind, the one where you felt very confident. 'See' it as if you were watching it on a screen (such as a TV screen or at the cinema). As you watch the inspired and confident you, hone in on the detail. What are you wearing? What colour are your clothes/shoes? What is going on in the background? Who else is speaking? Can you smell and odour or perfume? Are you holding anything in your hands or touching anything? Do you feel hungry or have you just eaten? Try to visualise as much data as possible and create a rich picture in your mind.

4. Wallow for a moment in the splendour of being so utterly confident, so completely in control and happy.

5. Try to make this picture bigger and brighter than you ever thought possible. Experience the joy that you feel inside and tell yourself how good it would be to be able to feel like this forever.

6. Now, at the height of your emotion, squeeze your thumb and forefinger on one hand together. This will provide an anchor for the feeling, to enable you to recreate it later.

7. Relax back, mentally turn the picture off and taking three deep breaths, open your eyes.

You will need to repeat this exercise regularly (at least ten times) to hard wire this zone into your regular thinking. Then, whenever you need to access that feeling, you simply press your thumb and forefinger together, and you will be back in the zone, experiencing all the feelings that you imagined. This recall will give you instant confidence to ensure that right from the beginning, when you enter the assessment centre, you are thinking like a winner.

I have used these techniques both on myself and with others and it truly is possible to rewire your inner thought patterns to enable you to experience more from life.

If you would like more information on zone thinking and also a free recording to help you fight your nerves and relax, download a complimentary copy simply by registering at www.growingu.com – and take a positive step towards being in charge of your life.

CHAPTER 3
PSYCHOMETRICS

Doesn't everyone want to know a bit more about the real person they are considering employing? How they think? Where their values lie? How they like to be motivated? How they like to make decisions?

Ever since the beginning of time, sages and scholars have been fascinated not only with ways to find out these aspects of our personalities but also categorising them into types or boxes. In ancient times there were considered four main types of temperaments:

- Sanguine – impulsive, pleasure seeking, sociable, forgetful, almost shameless
- Phlegmatic- relaxed, quiet, possibly sluggish, accepting, affectionate, rational, curious
- Choleric – ambitious, aggressive, energetic, passionate, potentially depressive
- Melancholic – introverted, thoughtful, creative, perfectionist, self reliant

These types were thought to be based on the preponderance of either too much or too little of inner body fluids, namely:

- Sanguine – blood
- Phlegmatic – phlegm
- Choleric – yellow bile
- Melancholic – black bile

Although we no longer use these categories some of the words still remain in our language today, such as describing someone as 'melancholy' or 'sanguine.'

However, although these measures may have moved on, the basic need to seek knowledge about someone and categorise them still remains, and this is the background to psychometrics.

WHAT ARE PSYCHOMETRICS?

The term 'psychometrics' is the collective name for tests or activities that can be undertaken to gain insight into your personality and your abilities. Sometimes you may undertake them yourself so that you can gain more self knowledge for your own personal development. Other times you may be asked to undertake them as part of an assessment of you to provide an insight into whether you would be the right candidate for a job or promotion.

Important point: all psychometric tests are undertaken by you. They therefore reflect your impression of you. They are not your manager's view or you or your colleague's view of you, and they have to be read in that context. For example, consider the example below:

Score nearer to 1 if you do not agree, and nearer to 5 if you strongly agree with the statement

I am a very confident person	1 2 3 4 5

If you feel you lack confidence, you may answer 1 or 2. If you have been brought up not to boast or push yourself forward you many answer 2 or 3. Even some very confident people may respond at 4 because giving yourself a 5 may seem a little extreme. However, if you are super confident then 5 might seem a reasonable score (hey, where's the 6?!) What would you choose?

Can you see that all this is very subjective, and is based on your thoughts and feelings about the question (what does it mean?) and how you should answer it (what does that say about you? Do you appear too brash/ demure – what impression does that give?) There is no mention here of how your current manager sees you or the view of your colleagues - it is based purely on your own assessment of you.

Look at the example again and imagine that you gave yourself a 3 (nice and safe, the middle number) but perhaps your manager would have chosen a 4. How is that of any use? Surely they can't both be a correct interpretation of you?

This is where we have to accept that the use of psychometrics only tells us half the story. There is no right answer or truth with psychometrics, what we look for is insight and tendencies, not judgement and definition. It may seem strange but the huge value in using psychometrics is not always in the report or answers but in the conversation that follows the tests. It is at these meetings that you really learn about the person, what mode of thought they were in when they undertook the tests, how they feel about the interpretation of their responses, and whether they think those interpretations are true of them. The interpretation is critical and that is why all psychometric tests should be administered by someone qualified to do so.

Note: if an organisation is using a free test from the internet, this is not credible as it has not gone through the rigorous tests that determine that it is both valid and reliable, and no one will have been trained to interpret the results or deal with any anomalies that may occur.

WHY ARE PSYCHOMETRICS USED?

At this point you will be forgiven for wondering why psychometrics are used at all. After all if they don't tell you the absolute truth about people or offer the tester an irrefutable insight to your personality what is the point?

Well psychometrics provide you (and the interviewer) with an insight as to how you are likely to react in certain situations, perhaps when you are under pressure, and how you prefer to think, which can be useful in areas such as decision making. For example you may be a very measured decision maker or perhaps you are more impulsive. There are pros and cons to each and a certain style may be preferred by an employer for that particular post. It also opens up a conversation with you around how and why you selected the answers you did, and if you do disagree with the profile it offers you – the candidate – an opportunity to explain why you selected that option and whether you feel it describes you.

Just a point to note here. Psychometrics are never used as the final decider in an assessment. That would not stand up under current Employment Law as psychometrics are not sufficiently accurate as evidence to be given in court, but in an assessment centre they can inform and confirm other behaviours displayed through the other exercises.

CAN YOU FAKE THE ANSWERS?

If you think about the traditional interview process rationally, it is fraught with problems. You can say anything in the interview and lay claim to work that was not yours, or bring along samples of work that are not your own. As you can see there is a lot of trust involved on the part of the interviewer to believe what you say and accept the examples of your work. So of course you can answer any of the questions in a psychometric test in any way you want. You can pretend that you are more outgoing and gregarious, just as you can fake the answers in an interview. We could all claim to be brilliant at everything, and when it comes to supplying names for references, why would you ever put forward the name for a reference of someone who felt your work was not good? Can you fake the answers? – Yes of course you can! However that might be a rather foolish way to go forward.

Although you may decide to put forward a more glowing view of yourself, there is one thing you will never know, and that is what the interviewer is looking for, and it is for that reason that it is best to answer honestly. I once had a colleague who went for a job as a manager in a large sales department. He thought that sales required a larger than life character and played up to this in his interview and answered all the psychometric tests to give that impression. Unfortunately for him they were not looking for anyone with that specific profile and were really seeking a candidate who was more thoughtful and precise. The job was for a manager of a sales team that was full of highly extroverts, and they really did not want a manager cut from the same cloth. They were looking for someone with a calmer and more steadying influence. Had he represented himself truthfully, he would have stood a greater chance of success. You see you cannot always tell exactly what the company are looking for. Of course a further problem would be that, had he been offered the job he would have had to keep up the pretence ad infinitum, and that is something that would have been very stressful. Nobody could keep pretending another personality forever, without it causing them extreme stress.

I hope I have convinced you to play strictly by the rules and answer honestly. If you are not what the company are looking for, then it will be better for you in the long run not to have secured that job, and to find another that is more suited to your talents and personality.

WHAT IF ENGLISH IS NOT MY FIRST LANGUAGE?

If the organisation is using one of the main and highly reputable psychometric tests, they will be available in other languages at no additional cost. Unfortunately many of the cheaper or 'off the shelf' products will only be available in the language within which it has been written.

If you take the test in another language you need to know that the test itself is not different, it is just the language that is different (for example using sidewalk instead of pavement). It does not change the meaning of the question. Therefore someone undertaking the US version of a test paper will undertake the same questions, simply adjusted for their understanding and comfort.

What different types of Psychometrics are there?

There are many ways to describe the different type of tests available but to keep everything simple I have divided them into four main groups:

- Ability tests
- Personality profile
- Intelligence tests/problem solving
- Specific test for certain jobs

Let's look at each one in turn and find out more about them.

ABILITY TESTS

Ability tests are put in place to test your ability to do a certain task. For example if you applied for a job as a bookkeeper, you may sit in the interview and tell me in great detail stunning stories of how you saved your current company from financial ruin. However, in reality that may have been your colleague or manager and perhaps you are just fooling yourself into thinking that you were the one to save the company, but how would I know? The best way for me to see just how good a bookkeeper you are is to see you actually analyse a spreadsheet or some company accounts. An ability test that allows you to show me the level of your skill would be a fantastic backup to your claims.

Perhaps you are looking for a job as a secretary and again you tell me that you can type at a speed of 90 words per minute. Can you really? A typing test would be just the thing to show your skill and this is again another form of ability test.

Ability tests can be anything from showing that you can screw the top on a tube of toothpaste to sitting a mathematical exam to demonstrate your dexterity with numbers. It can take the form of someone observing you doing something or a test paper. If it is in a paper format, these can be bought freely from shops, testing companies, and online, and the employer does not have to hold any qualification to administer one to potential employees or staff. The most important point here is that the test is applicable to the job. For example if you were applying to be a hairdresser, you would be expected to demonstrate your skills but being given a mathematical paper that deals with sophisticated transactions (such as changing currency) would be inappropriate. However a job for an import/ export clerk may indeed require a demonstration of currency transactions and calculations.

Some ability tests will be in the form of sitting a questionnaire or test paper and others may be an activity. A test paper will be knowledge based with questions such as:

How much is 34% of £32.50?

or,

If you get 3800 roomlas to a sezzar and 0.3 sezzars to a pound, how many roomlas will you get for £5.75?

Both of these questions require numerical knowledge and dexterity (and by the way, the answer is £11.05 and 6,555 roomlas)

An activity can be somewhat different. I gave you the example earlier of a typing test, but another commonly used example is that of an in tray exercise, which we will cover later in this book.

HOW TO PREPARE FOR AN ABILITY TEST

1. Stay calm – you should only be asked to undertake tests that link to the job on offer.

2. Look at the job description for your job and pick out the verbs (the 'doing' words) and actions such as 'type at 30 words per minute' or 'maintain a budget sheet.'

3. Unpick that a little further if necessary, if more all encompassing words are used such as 'manage' what does that actually mean? What skills would you need to manage? How would you demonstrate those?

4. Write a list of aspects that would make you credible or give evidence that you can do that action.

5. Consider how you would test that out, if you wanted to run an assessment centre for that job.

6. Remember that you can practise and prepare. Read books, sit other papers, practice your typing, refresh your memory regarding equations – and so forth.

7. Practice any free ability tests that you can find online and make sure you complete them in time, and up skill yourself on obvious basic maths such as percentages and ratios.

An example is on the following page.

JOB TITLE: MANAGER FOR NEW TEAM IN A FACTORY		
Taken from the Job Description	**What this actually means (a breakdown)**	**How this could be tested psychometrically**
Manage the team	Giving direction Motivating staff Leadership	In-tray activity Leadership questionnaire
Budget management	Mathematical skills IT skills	Mathematical test paper Computer task Both together in an online test paper
Writing reports	Communication Written writing skills	Language and grammar test paper An in-tray exercise including a written report
Time management	Completing tasks on time Reaching deadlines	In-tray exercise around priorities In-try exercise that includes planning Completion of all the tests within the timeframe

Now complete a form for your job (continue on a separate sheet if you need more space)

JOB TITLE:		
Taken from the Job Description	**What this actually means (a breakdown)**	**How this could be tested psychometrically**

PERSONALITY PROFILE

Personality profiling is big business, and whatever your personal feelings about these psychometric tests, employers feel that they add to the recruitment and assessment process and therefore you should expect to have to complete one for most jobs (especially supervisor level and above).

Personality profiling is aimed at finding out whether you fit into the organisation and how you operate. Some organisations are highly driven and want staff who score high on ambition and drive, whereas other organisations run more as a cooperative and are looking for more cooperative employees, who are willing to sacrifice their own ideas and glory for the good of the whole team. These are extreme examples but I am sure you can see that someone who fits the first category would be frustrated in an organisation offering the second setting.

Traditionally personality profiling centres around what is known as the Big Five personality traits. These are traits that have been studied for many years and have been found to be reliable to test (in other words they can be tested fairly accurately on different people and gain reliable results) and consistent in that they don't suddenly change within most people's lifetimes. For example, someone who is an extrovert is not likely to change to become introvert unless they have undergone some life changing experience. The Big Five are:

- Extroversion – the amount to which you like to gain energy from the outside world, integrating and sharing ideas

- Neuroticism/anxiety – this aims to measure how excited or anxious you become around work tasks

- Openness to experience/conformity – this aims to measure whether you are a 'corporate beast' or a 'maverick'

- Agreeableness/tender versus tough mindedness – aims to measure the extent to which you follow others and are able to take decisions independently

- Conscientiousness – this is the amount to which you are able to focus on your work and pay attention to detail.

Have a quick look through that list and think that if each one was depicted as on a line, where would you be on that line?

Can you see that some jobs and some organisations might want very different types of people? Further that if the fit is not a good one, then you could find the job or workplace very stressful? For example someone with a high score in neuroticism/anxiety might find that they are driven to complete distraction by a job that relies on detail and deadlines. A person who prefers conformity at work may feel very uncomfortable in a loosely managed company that values feedback on experience rather than being given direction. An employee who has a high level of agreeableness and likes to 'keep the peace' may struggle when told that they are expected to get tough and make all the decisions themselves. Finally we all have differences in how much detail we put into our work, and perfectionists do not always work well with those that prefer a broad brush approach.

These Big Five are only the beginning and most personality tests will ascertain these and many other personality factors that sit together, to give an outline of the person and provide insight for the assessors.

Traditionally personality profiles were completed with a pen and paper in a test situation but now it is more likely that you will be sent a link via email and you complete the test online. There are three critical things that you need to remember:

1. However much you are tempted, never get anyone else to complete the test for you. Be honest and complete it yourself. If your profile is contrary to the employers needs, you would not be happy there and would probably leave anyway, and further, it would be embarrassing to be asked at an interview why you answered a question in a certain way when in the other activities you behaved in a completely different way.

2. Concentrate and complete the task in one sitting. The computer is not only registering your responses, it is counting how long you take. If you leave the test midway to have a chat or go and make a drink, your results will be flagged up as 'odd' and you will be questioned about this at the assessment centre. Neither should you be too fast – a paper of around 120 questions should take you about 20-40 minutes to complete. If you take 10 minutes there is a danger that you have not read and considered the questions sufficiently and if you took over an hour, it may indicate that you are either not taking the test seriously (and you went off to do something else) or that perhaps you were trying to research the 'right answer' online or by asking others.

3. There are no right or wrong answers. A personality test is not there to find out whether you are an axe-wielding mad person or murderer, it is just about fit – and you will have an opportunity to discuss the outcome and disagree with it if you feel it is not a fair representation of you.

HOW TO PREPARE FOR A PERSONALITY PROFILE

1. Look at the job description and the person specification. What type of person are they looking for? A team player? Someone who works well on their own? A manager? A leader?

2. Be honest – are you that person? For example, if it is a senior position, how do you manage your stress levels?

3. Envisage the type of person the organisation wants to employ. The responses you give will need to reflect this.

4. Undertake some desktop research on the psychometric paper. You can easily find out what the paper measures.

5. If you are undertaking the test in advance of the assessment centre, find a time when you can totally concentrate on the task and ask not to be disturbed.

6. If you are completing the profile at home, make sure you are thinking in work mode. We can be different at home and this may come through otherwise.

7. Practice any free personality tests that you can find online and make sure you complete them in time. Try using your search engine by typing in 'free psychometric tests' or similar.

INTELLIGENCE TESTS/PROBLEM SOLVING

Intelligence tests have been around for a long time but I am also going to add in this section problem solving and logical tests. These tests tend to measure specific things. They are not about personality but reward logical and ordered thinking. Current research tells us that there are many different types of intelligence, not just numerical and logical but these tests are enduring and seem to be forever popular when wishing to gauge the mechanics of project management or senior management. They do not provide any data regarding relationships towards others (for example they would not show whether you are empathic with people) but they indicate a certain type of linear thinking that is valued in many quarters.

Intelligence or problem solving tests can be practiced as many of the same questions will come up time and time again. Even if you do not have exactly the same question, the technique for solving it will be similar. In a pattern recognition paper (ones that ask you 'Which shape or pattern comes next in this sequence?') the questions will form into types, and when you learn the trick of each type, you can solve most of them fairly easily. For example if I told you to look at a sequence of similar pictures and notice first of all the shape around the outside, then at the length of the two lines within, because one of them is sure to have one line nearer the other or shorter, then you would be able to apply this approach to any similar diagrammatic problem in the future. It is very similar to crosswords. If you always buy the same newspaper or magazine and regularly do the crossword you will find that you get better and faster at solving it, and funnily enough, sometimes the same clue will come up for the same word. This is because they are very often written by the same person or small group of writers and you simply start to learn how they think. Once you lock into their thinking pattern, you can anticipate their clues and responses. For this reason, practice and repetition can take you a long way with these tests.

HOW TO PREPARE FOR AN INTELLIGENCE OR PROBLEM SOLVING TEST

1. Look at the job description. What type of planning or financial skills are you expected to have? Do you need to be a logical thinker and have a methodical approach?

2. Research online or buy a book on how to solve these tests. You are doing no more than undertaking research and giving yourself more confidence.

3. Create a fun attitude around these tests – see them as similar to Suduko books or puzzles from inside crackers. If you make them fun you will learn more successfully.

4. Try to undertake similar tests and time yourself. Put yourself under pressure by reducing the time of the paper by five minutes.

5. If you get a question wrong, use this as a learning pointer. Find out how the solution can be found so that you know the technique for the future.

6. Search the internet for examples and free practice papers. The more you practice the easier they become.

7. If you are finding it tough, remember that this only demonstrates one way of thinking and will not account for the entire assessment.

SPECIFICALLY FOCUSED TESTS FOR CERTAIN JOBS

I have already mentioned that some personality tests have been in existence for a very long time and are therefore considered reliable and fair. However, these are general indicators of our whole personality. Some test manufacturers over the past sixty years have taken this a step further and developed tests that look at specific areas or skills that are needed for certain situations or job roles. By specific areas I mean:

- Team types – these assess your place in the team and the strengths and weaknesses of that role

- Preferences – these assess your preferred way of working or learning (the importance here is that they do not claim that you cannot work in any other way, only that you would find it stressful to work against your preference)

- Emotional intelligence – these tests assess your level of emotional intelligence and the amount to which you feel in control of your emotions

... and many more. There are also psychometric tests that claim to be written specifically to collect information that pertains to certain skills sets required for particular jobs such as psychometric tests for:

- Sales staff
- Customer service staff
- Managers

Finally there are the more playful, and less rigorously tested psychometrics aimed at learning while having fun:

- What dog type are you?

- What flower are you?

- What's your flavour?

As you can see, apart from the final sets (which are mainly for fun) there is often a set of psychometrics available for every situation, although some are less reliable, and could be contested.

HOW TO PREPARE FOR SPECIFICALLY FOCUSED TESTS

1. In the first instance consider what the test is (the clue is usually in the title). If the company are investing in this they must believe it is important. For example if they are asking you to take a team type test they obviously believe that team work is very important.

2. Relax and be yourself in the test, but do look out for certain obvious questions. For example, if you are undertaking a team type test and you reply 'no' to the statement 'I like working in teams' and 'yes' to a further statement 'I prefer to work alone' –you only have yourself to blame!

3. Remember that your responses will be checked out against your behaviour at the assessment centre and they should be consistent.

4. All psychometric tests ask the same question several times to check that you are consistent in your replies, therefore try to be otherwise the computer will flag up those inconsistencies.

5. Practice a range of similar tests online so that you feel comfortable.

6. Take your time and read all the questions fully. Try not to leave any questions out no matter how hard that might be.

7. Note that most psychometrics ask you a 'trick' statement such as 'I never tell a lie' or 'I have never been late.' These are to demonstrate whether you are trying to portray yourself in a better light to the tester and will cause the tester to question all of your responses. The answer is that at some time we have all told lies and been late – therefore answer 'no' if you are asked whether those statements are true of you.

WHAT ARE THEY LOOKING FOR?

I mentioned earlier that when it comes to psychometric testing, you will never know EXACTLY what the assessors are looking for, and that is certainly true of personality profiles, but let's look at some assumptions you can happily make.

If you undertake some basic research you can find out in advance about the company (if it is not your current organisation) and gain some feel for the culture. Ask yourself:

- Is it competitive?
- Do they consider personal values to be of high importance?
- Do they prefer a more aggressive style of action or someone more laid back?
- What sort of style do they prefer for decisions? Collaborative? Autocratic?
- Are they looking for charismatic, outwardly confident individuals?
- What exactly are people there valued for?

These questions will give you an idea of the type of person they will be looking for and the traits that they will want to see, and there may be a list of competencies on the company website. Of course this does not mean that it is a sure done deal that this is what they are looking for (they may be looking for a complete change of culture), but organisations rarely take the extraordinary step of trying to change the world overnight, especially in terms of employee recruitment. They may want to soften the edges but a complete turnaround would be radical in the least, and therefore I am sure you can use their competencies as a guide.

Let's make some more assumptions based on what we know. If you are applying for a job in management it helps to have some 'people' skills and to be able to motivate others. There would also be the expectation of a certain level of confidence both in your decisions and in practical matters such as how you pull together a report or a presentation. Most employers today are also looking for staff that show a willingness to learn and develop. Flexibility is also key and rigidity is so yesterday!

Finally, take a good look at yourself and be honest. Do you fit? Are you asking them to take a risk? Are you selling yourself short? Assessors want to see the best that you can offer and therefore it is worth putting some effort into ensuring you have prepared and are not caught out.

FEEDBACK

Best practice is that, after giving up your time and energy to expose your inner self through psychometrics, you should receive some form of feedback. Feedback on psychometrics and tests comes in two forms, one beneficial to you and the other to the employer:

1. To provide you with learning points for the future

2. To confirm that how you report through the tests is accurate.

Let's look at the first reason. If you do not fit the profile of the person they are looking for, it can be helpful to know where they believe you fall short. It is also helpful to find out where they believe your strengths lay for the future. These points can be developmental for your career in general, but this becomes critical should you want to try for the position again. (Some assessment centres automatically stream their feedback into the individual's development profile or appraisal documentation, via their manager).

The second point I have alluded to earlier. Psychometric tests are not fully proven. You could lie throughout, you could misrepresent yourself accidentally, you could find a colleague to sit the test for you, or you could drift off and be in 'home mode' the entire time. All through the assessment process all the behaviours you exhibit will be cross checked to gauge reliability, for example if your psychometric states that you are assertive, and in your feedback you agree with that, assertive behaviour will be sought for throughout all the other activities. It is therefore important that the psychometric test(s) represent you accurately. During the feedback you will be asked several times whether the report feels like a good representation of you, and if you say 'no' then it is your opportunity to explain why and explore how you came to give the response to those particular questions that contributed towards that outcome. This is your chance to set the record straight if it needs to be done.

Finally, it is always recommended that the feedback is undertaken by a person qualified in the particular brand of psychometric used. The reason for this is that they understand how the test is put together, its nuances, and how certain aspects can be interpreted. It is not usually recommended that the manager gives the feedback, unless they are fully trained.

There is a whole chapter devoted to feedback in chapter 9 of this book.

CHAPTER 4
IN-TRAY
EXERCISES

Now we move onto the activities that make up an assessment centre day. Most of the psychometric tests will have been undertaken in advance and now it is for you to turn up on the day and undertake a number of activities that demonstrate your skills, knowledge and ability.

A very popular activity is the in-tray exercise. This is an activity that is designed to demonstrate how you make decisions and work through tasks. You may be thinking, well I thought they tested that through the psychometric questionnaire – and yes they probably did, but do you remember that I said that assessors need to see consistency? The assessors need to see you perform consistently across all the activities, and an in-tray exercise is a good way to gauge that your decision making is indeed consistent.

WHAT IS AN IN-TRAY EXERCISE?

It is an assessment activity that requires you to put a number of suggested activities in the order that you perceive they should take place. It is an attempt to simulate a business situation, and typically you play the part of the employee who has come in either first thing in the morning or to a first day in a job, and there is a list of activities and events that you need to tackle. You need to read each item and decide on the order and how you will deal with each item (you may be asked to give reasons for each selection.) Oh, and to put a little pressure on, there is usually a time limit.

The in-tray may contain:

- Letters of complaint
- General letters/correspondence
- Memos
- Emails
- Notes

.. and you will usually be given some information about the company and a calendar to help you.

(Just a note – some organisations are now incorporating e-tray exercises. These are exactly the same as in-tray exercises except that the information is given to you completely by email so that the exercise becomes computer-based.)

Have a go at the very simple example on the next page. I realise that you may not be a Deputy Head Teacher but using your common sense, what do you think should go first?

Put a '1' by the first activity you would undertake and '2' by the second until you have covered all the activities.

It is Monday morning, 10 June at 8.30 am. You arrive at your desk to find the following issues vying for you attention. You are the new Deputy Head Teacher at Manor Borough Primary School, and the Head Teacher is away for the week on a course. In what order would you prioritise the following tasks:

Item 1	Issue left on the desk – a message left by the Head asking you to proof read the final copy of the new school prospectus that is due at the printers ready for distribution at the start of the new term.
Item 2	Issue on desk – draft copy of a newsletter to go out to parents today about an event next week – the manuscript needs attention before passing to the Admin office
Item 3	Fax – arrived through at 8.25 from Social Services about a child protection issue with regards to a student in Year 2 that has arisen during the last couple of days. Social Services want an urgent response.
Item 4	Phone call comes in from a supply teacher that you had engaged to cover the Head's teaching duties – "Sorry can't come in, I'm off sick."
Item 5	Phone message from the finance officer to remind the Head that the budget return is overdue and is needed by 12 noon today.
Item 6	The Head has left you his/her password and has asked that you make sure that the Head Teacher inbox is emptied of emails every day, and that each one is dealt with on the day it comes in. The mail box is currently showing 30 messages.
Item 7	Following a knock at the door the caretaker enters to report on a serious broken glass problem in a classroom as a result of vandalism the previous evening.
Item 8	You hear shouting in the corridor – it sounds like a parent that wants to speak with the Head and they sound angry.
Item 9	The post contains a letter of resignation from a Learning Assistant who cites bullying by the class teacher with whom she normally works. She is at work this morning.
Item 10	In the post is an offer of free trips to a summer school for disadvantaged year one children – but applications need to be in immediately.
Item 11	The door opens and in comes Andy Cappel a local authority officer who was just passing by and thought he would drop in to see how the refurbishments on the school are going.

Morning assembly starts at 9.15 am and although its organisation is in the hands of the Rainbow class, the Head or Deputy is always present.

HOW DID YOU DO? WAS IT DAUNTING?

It should not have been too bad because this is a fairly simple and straightforward version of an in-tray activity.

Did you notice that some of the items were more urgent than others, and some were demanding a more immediate response. Of course just because someone is demanding a quick response does not mean that you have to give them one.

Remember that there is no right answer to this as long as you justify every stage. Here is what I would do, but yours may differ:

Order	Reasoning
1	Item 3 – this has warnings all over it 'Child Protection,' 'Social services' – there could be a child in danger and if it were to come to court, you would need to account for your reason for delaying – therefore act immediately.
2	Item 2 – broken glass requires immediate action (health and safety) and the police would need to be called regarding the vandalism
3	Item 8 – I would ask the parent to take a seat in reception and offer them a drink. Often when irate people wait for a few minutes their anger dissipates – but I could only leave this parent for a few minutes.
4	Item 9 – I would ask the teacher concerned to come to my office and tell them that I would like to speak with them fully at break time. I would then excuse them from duties for the morning as there could be an investigation later that day. (Depending on the severity of the accusation I might send them home and tell them that I will be in touch). Bullying is a serious accusation.
5	Item 11 – Explain briefly your problem and ask Mr Cappel to make an appointment to come back later in the day or the week.
6	Item 2 - the newsletter must go out today otherwise there will be insufficient notice for parents to attend the event. It should only take a moment to read through and this task could be delegated.

7	Item 4 – I have left this down the list because there is probably nothing that can be done today anyway. At my earliest availability I would ring the supply agency and request another candidate for tomorrow (or ask them to deal with the situation).
8	Item 5 – after I had spoken to the parent, I would ring the finance office and see whether there is some leeway on the budget timetable. If there isn't, I would deal with it here and send it off.
9	Item 1 – it is not clear whether this is important for today or the size of it but it probably could be done this evening and sent to the printers tomorrow.
10	Item 6 – you could place this one higher up the ranking if you want, or mention that you would scan the subject headings early on, but emails are quickest answered in one sitting, and you will probably have some time later that day.
11	Item 10 – this is lovely but needs some thought. You will need to prove fairness in this situation and probably involve the teachers. Do not be pushed into their timetable because it could cause you problems if you try to rush your response.

Important point: don't forget the assembly. It may not be an item but what would you do?

There are some items that could be done in parallel, some that could have been pushed even further down the list (such as item 11), some you need to make assumptions about (item 4), and some you do not know how complex the situation might be (item 8). This is why you need to justify and explain your actions.

WHAT DO IN-TRAY EXERCISES TEST?

In an in-tray exercise test, the assessors are looking for:

- Your ability to take in and process information
- Your capacity for analysing problems and looking ahead to future repercussions
- How you make decisions under pressure and prioritise effectively
- Your ability to be creative
- How you assess possible problems
- How effective you are at implementing solutions
- How you manage time effectively
- How you deal with people tactfully
- Your ability to delegate some tasks
- Your knowledge as to when it is appropriate that you respond personally
- Your ability to consider the wider implications for the organisation
- How you negotiate and/or influence others

An important point here (and mentioned previously) is that, there is very little real actual right and wrong with these lists, and we could spend ages arguing whether a certain activity is number 14 or 15, and some of this will relate to any real life experiences that you may have had. For example if you had an experience where dealing with a complaint before a member of staff went terribly wrong, then you might give it much more priority (because you would not want it to go wrong again). Similarly if you found that the way you handled it last time was perfect, then you would place it lower down the list.

So, if it is not conclusive and we can't even all agree on an exact order, why would they ask you to do it then? What is the point? The assessor is simply wanting to see that you understand the main principles of prioritising and that you are able to justify your order. If you can, then fine. There are key activities (perhaps five or six) that really do need to come within the top third, then a medium set, and finally a low priority set. It can be a good way of thinking of it:

1. High priority   2. Medium priority   3. Low priority

SO, HOW SHOULD YOU BE UNDERTAKING THIS TASK TO ENSURE GREAT RESULTS?

Let's look first at some quick preliminaries.

Firstly read carefully through all the paper work you are given. Look at the company background or consider any information given as important to the decisions you are about to make (for example in the school situation, the head teacher has a duty of care to the children as well as to staff). Important point: the tests do not provide background information for nothing. If you are told that severe rain is forecast, then this is an important point that you are expected to take into consideration and WILL come up. No surprise then when one of the 'problems' is a leaking roof or a scheduled sports day! In my example did you notice the comment about assembly at the very bottom of the list. You would be expected to build this point into your decision.

If you are provided with an organisational chart, notice who is in which job. It can make a difference in how you respond in a given situation. Also note the dates. A complaint letter that is four days old may become suddenly far more urgent. In our Deputy Head Teacher example, you are given the date so that you can judge where you are in relation to the beginning of the next term (item 1).

Follow the written instructions carefully. Some exercises will just ask you to place the activities in order, some will ask you to complete a diary. Others may ask you to provide written explanations for each decision and then again some may ask you to start drafting replies to the respondents or write what you will actually do in each situation. Also check out the time limit and make sure you allocate sufficient time for each part of the task.

Make a rough plan and note how you are going to undertake the exercise. Now read through ALL the examples and make notes or highlight certain words that you need to remember.

Go through the example again and put a 1, 2 or 3 in the boxes to indicate whether you think them high, medium or low priority.

Now look at the situations in each category. For each category try to place them on the grid below:

	Important	Not so important
Urgent	1	2
Not urgent	3	4

The items that you think may be urgent (perhaps they present a risk?) need to be balanced against their level of importance. For example if someone is standing in front of you with blood dripping from their hand because of an accident, that would feature in box one because it is both urgent and important. It needs to be dealt with now and fast.

However if a colleague rings up and tells you that they are off sick, but when you look on their timetable, they have no classes scheduled for the rest of the week, as long as there is no problem with cover, it is an urgent issue, but not so important in terms of your timeframe. It might therefore go in box two.

Now consider that the colleague who is off sick was meant to be writing a report regarding summer activities at the school during this week. It is important for the school because it is how you raise money, but it is not that urgent and could be written when she comes back to school, that would feature in section three.

Finally there is the birthday rota to sort out. When all hands are 'to the pump' that is not very urgent or important. It could certainly be done next week, and therefore it would feature in section four.

(One final little tip here is to not go for the quickest remedies in a misguided view of knocking off five or six activities in the first ten minutes. Always consider safety first, an accident, broken glass or electrical failing – anything that puts people in danger. Secondly consider the time angle – what has to be actioned immediately? Then move all less urgent requests to the end, such as a request for holiday time off. That leaves you with the central activities and you simply have to think them through).

If you remember the first tip of putting all activities into three main 'piles' – then the order within those piles could be up for debate but to place an activity that really should be urgent and important low down the list would certainly call your expertise into question.

ACTION AND TIMING

There will be a time limit because an in-tray exercise is supposed to put you under pressure. After all, you would need to make decisions if you were in a working environment, and this is what it aims to simulate.

Stay calm and if there is not sufficient information, you may have to make some assumptions. This is a normal part of life and something we do every day. You will not be marked down on this unless your assumption is completely off the wall. For example, if you decide to write to someone who has sent in a complaint, I think the assumption that they are annoyed would be justified. The assumption that they are happy and satisfied would simply be bizarre, and considered strange behaviour.

If you are asked to give your actions, work through in a logical order from the most urgent onwards. That way if you don't reach the end in time, you will have dealt with the main issues. Just check that the order flows (in your planning) before you start writing. Some activities may be dependent on others (for example your caretaker cannot be cleaning up glass if he is the person off sick). Some activities may also take place simultaneously (such as delegating tasks). Give reasons for your decisions wherever you can.

While we are mentioning delegation, check in the text that it does not say that you have to do everything yourself. Look on the organisation chart – do you have a secretary? An assistant? An administrator? A deputy or second in command? What actions could be allocated to them?

MOVING ON

Ready for a more challenging exercise?

Great!

I mentioned to you that the example given here was very simple. If you are applying for a management position, expect the in-tray exercise to reflect the job and the company. Therefore let's look at our BabyMaxPro case study at the back of this book. Read it through again.

Done that?

You have been brought in as interim manager at BabyMaxPro – consider the following items:

Item 1	You have just received an email telling you of industrial action at Lincoln Pharmaceuticals. This is the third case threatened this year.
Item 2	There has been a break-in at the Babymax Pro offices. Only one computer has gone missing.
Item 3	You have feedback that your budget figures are incorrect and there is a board meeting in 20 minutes.
Item 4	Your assistant (a temp) has called in sick with a headache. It is the second time this has happened in two weeks.
Item 5	You have an email from an angry customer claiming that BabyMax Pro has caused a rash on their child.
Item 6	John Brown, one of your staff members, has just announced that the fortnight's leave he is just about to take is his honeymoon! He has been with you for ten years and leaves at midday today. There really ought to be a present for him and his new bride-to-be.
Item 7	You have just received an email from a journalist in Australia informing you that toys similar to those in the Learning Range have been seen on sale in Australia under the brand name 'Kismet' – and that company has Paul Dickinson as director.
Item 8	You have just heard that Stephen Leeming (a guest at the board meeting) has broken down in his car, approximately 15 minutes from the offices.
Item 9	Jan Foreman from Today (a top newspaper) rings to request an interview. She would like the interview to go in the weekend supplement and would like to meet you later today.
Item 10	Jane Pickles comes in to tell you that money has gone missing from the charity fund jar on her desk. She is very upset.
Item 11	An inspector from the Health and Safety organisation is waiting in reception. He decided to do a spot check.

Create the order that you would undertake these items in and justify why.

Tip: don't forget the techniques explained earlier (high, medium, low and the urgent important grid).

There is a space below for your final answer.

Order	Reasoning
1	
2	
3	
4	
5	
6	
7	
8	
9	
10	
11	

OK, how did you find that? It is not that easy is it? But it helps when you can justify your order with an explanation.

As I keep mentioning, there is no right answer to any in-tray exercise but there are issues that each of these items raise, and it helps to consider these. Not in priority order, I have listed my thoughts below and of course you may have thought of some more.

Item 1   You have just received an email telling you of industrial action at Lincoln Pharmaceuticals. This is the third case threatened this year.

The issues here is that BabyMaxPro are thinking of moving their manufacturing business to Lincoln Pharmaceuticals. Given the level of staff unrest, is this still a good idea. Should this be reported to the Board? Although this is not urgent there is a Board meeting this morning and you may want to place this on the agenda. There certainly needs more investigation (you will need to remind everyone of facts such as how much longer your contract with your current manufacturer will run; you must not leave the company without a supplier).

Item 2   There has been a break-in at the Babymax Pro offices. Only one computer has gone missing.

This is a police issue and must be reported immediately. Are you sure that only one computer has gone (sometimes smaller items such as mobile phones or documents are not missed until later). The computer is not really the big issue here. What information was on the computer? Was the information backed up? Is this also a company security issue? Why was the building not secure? You will also need to contact your insurance company. (The purchase of a replacement computer could be delegated). These dealings can all be very time consuming.

Item 3	You have feedback that your budget figures are incorrect and there is a Board meeting in 20 minutes.
	This is urgent and important both for the business and for your career. Calculating figures incorrectly shows a lack of professionalism and attention to detail. This is made even worse by large decisions being made on the back of them! You need to correct these as a matter of urgency, even if it means asking if the item considering budget is moved down the agenda – perhaps giving you an additional hour.
Item 4	Your assistant (a temp) has called in sick with a headache. It is the second time this has happened in two weeks.
	Try to delegate this task for now. Ask someone to find you another temp – then later take this up with the agency. If they procrastinate, you need to consider working with another agency. You need to know that you have reliable staff. (Just as a matter in point, you also need to consider whether there may be an issue in the workplace. Ink and photocopy fumes can cause headaches – are your rooms well ventilated? You have a duty of care to all staff who work for you, whether they are temporary or permanent).
Item 5	You have an email from an angry customer claiming that BabyMax Pro has caused a rash on their child.
	This is both important and urgent. The way you respond could strengthen or jeopardise your case should there be a legal case. Therefore it needs careful handling and a complete investigation. You do not want the customers to go to the newspapers saying that you have not responded or ignored them. For now send a quick holding email, telling the writer that you are very concerned and that you need to investigate and come back to them. Put this in your diary to do either later that day or first thing tomorrow.

Item 6	John Brown, one of your staff members has just announced that the fortnight's leave he is just about to take is his honeymoon! He has been with you for ten years and leaves at midday today. There really ought to be a present for him and his new bride-to-be.
	Maintaining staff morale and harmony is hugely important. Although this has been sprung upon you, he has worked at the company a long time. Make a quick calculation (for example £2 per head of general staff, £5 (or more) from more senior staff) and delegate someone to buy a voucher from a main store, to be presented at lunchtime, when he leaves. You could even organise an online voucher in two minutes. If you want to ask for the money back from everyone – do that later. The most important thing here is to honour your staff member. Staff goodwill is worth more than a few pounds.
Item 7	You have just received an email from a journalist in Australia informing you that toys similar to those in the Learning Range have been seen on sale in Australia under the brand name 'Kismet' – and that company has Paul Dickinson as director.
	This might sound urgent but it could be scaremongering. You need to take your time on this one by first going back to Paul's contract. Does it specifically say that you have international rights or patent on the toys? What was the agreement? When you have checked the details you would want to look into Kismet – who are they? What do they do? How is Paul associated? In other words all this is very important but needs to be actioned methodically and proof needs to be obtained before you even begin to speak with Paul. It is not an item that should be rushed through in one morning, and you should not be bothering the Board until you have all the facts.
Item 8	You have just heard that Stephen Leeming (a guest at the board meeting) has broken down in his car, approximately 15 minutes from the offices.
	Could this be delegated? Could someone drive out and collect him? Could his item be moved further down the agenda? Again this sounds urgent and worrying but actually it is quite easily fixable and the car can be dealt with later.

Item 9   Jan Foreman from Today (a top newspaper) rings to request an interview. She would like the interview to go in the weekend supplement and would like to meet you later today.

Take this seriously as journalists are known for producing copy whether you agree to be involved or not! Try to find out what the angle is on the story? Could the interview questions be emailed over instead? What about a telephone interview? (Be friendly) would she like any of your stock photos to illustrate the piece? If she insists it must be face to face (and you feel it is right to do it) schedule it for later in the day. It will give you time to think and plan – her urgent is not necessarily your urgent.

Item 10   Jane Pickles comes in to tell you that money has gone missing from the charity fund jar on her desk. She is very upset.

Could this be linked to the break in? Has anything else gone missing? Try to calm Jane down and give her something practical to do, such as undertake a quick inventory of the area, informal interviews from others, liaising with the police/insurance. Actions like this are very upsetting for staff. Hold an informal staff meeting later that day and discuss the issue – it could just be a mistake such as someone emptying the jar to store its contents somewhere more safely.

Item 11   An inspector from the Health and Safety organisation is waiting in reception. He decided to do a spot check.

This is important and urgent. Some organisations are allowed to undertake spot checks, and therefore check on the powers of the Health and Safety Executive. If this is correct then it is better to allow them to do so by guiding them to a particular part of your business and inviting them to start there. Inform the inspector of the theft issue, and apologise that it is taking up your time, offer them a drink, and allow them to get on with their business. If you try to obstruct or hide anything, you will look suspicious. Most inspectors are either doing an overall check (in which case they just want a quick look at everything and then rush back to type up their report), or in response to a complaint (in which case they will focus in on one aspect of your business in great detail). Therefore you will have a gut feeling as to why they are there. Unless you truly have something to hide, leave them to get on with their check or assign them another member of staff to be their contact, before meeting them again finally at the end of their visit.

To help you prepare for in-tray activities, consider the following:

1. Think about the job you are applying for, what content are you likely to be given in an in-tray exercise? (Notice that although my two examples are a Head in a school and a manager, some of the problems listed are very similar because people and premises issues occur in many jobs).

2. Remember that activities can be delegated if you have suitable staff (see the organisational chart if there is one).

3. Highlight any additional important information such as the date or time.

4. Make sure you do exactly what is asked of you. If you need to justify your thoughts – do that.

5. Use high, medium and low priority piles first and then prioritise within those.

6. Look for any links where two activities can be done at the same time, or conversely the same person cannot be in two places at the same time!

7. Never shirk (or delegate) your responsibility.

CHAPTER 5
GROUP ACTIVITIES

WHAT ARE GROUP ACTIVITIES?

Group activities are literally what they suggest – activities that take place in groups, and not on your own. The group size can be anything from 2 upwards and could be as many as thirty.

Group activities may also range from the cerebral (using the group to think) to the physical (and this could be anything from the less strenuous building a tower from spaghetti, to the more testing issue of swinging from ropes).

What is the purpose of group activities?

Group activities are included in an assessment centre to test how you perform within a group situation: how you decided on your place within the group and how you interact with others. Today it is accepted that mechanical skills and knowledge are not enough by themselves; they are only part of the story. Very few people work in isolation and the ability to work with others, motivate and tap into their idea streams are key, especially in management jobs where these skills are tested.

Group activities consider more than straight communication, they reveal:

- the dynamics that go on between people and how you react
- how you deal with conflict
- whether you can instigate ideas

- how obstructive you might be
- how you respond to the ideas of others
- whether you are a leader or follower
- the extent to which you are able to build on other ideas
- the amount to which you are compliant and willing to go with the group

These activities are therefore there to test or assess how you react in people-focussed situations and to put you under some form of pressure. We can all be on our best behaviour while the world is ordered and things are going well, but very often we revert to type under pressure. It is when we are under pressure that we see how short a person's temper really is, or how they handle discord in the group. Of course all this is not happening in isolation because you also need to perform within the group and solve a puzzle or situation, which again takes your eye off the ball and distracts you from concentrating on how you want to portray your behaviour.

When you take part in a group activity it is very likely that the observers will already have your psychometric assessment and will be looking at behaviour that either refutes or endorses what it says, and therefore group activities are a way of double-checking your skills and behaviour.

WHAT DO GROUP ACTIVITIES LOOK LIKE?

When you are asked to undertake a group activity you will be given a scenario and you may also be given roles – not quite, "You are Professor Green in the library," – more like, "You are the HR manager," – but you get the picture.

You are expected to conduct the meeting or take part in the activity in the role of that person and represent whatever company your role play asks of you. If you are given a role then be assured that everyone else will be too. You may also be given additional papers to read through.

You will then be asked to enter a room which is usually laid out with a largish area in the middle where you will enact the activity (there may be a table and chairs) and several chairs with their backs against the walls. The chairs against the wall, facing inwards, are for your observers, and they may even be sitting there when you enter the room. These observers are the assessors for this activity. They will be watching you intently throughout the activity and will mark significant facts regarding your comments, body language and behaviour on sheets of paper throughout the activity. Examples of these records are shown in Chapter 1. The observers will not speak to you throughout the entire activity and often remain in the room even after you have left. You may find that they do not even make eye contact with you; they endeavour to stay as neutral as possible.

Take a seat around the table (if there is one). It is also helpful to pretend that you do not know the other people present, so that you start with introductions. This enables you instantly to get to know who the other 'players' are in this part of the assessment centre, and who (and what) they are representing. From this you will begin to draw conclusions, for example it is likely that the Finance manager has some money and that others around the table will be competing for it – but keep an open mind, these are only tentative ideas at this stage.

Enact the activity as you would in real life. You will find that as you progress you will be drawn into the activity and this is where your real behaviour is shown, but it is best to try to remember that you are being assessed at all times.

Tip: try to read the competency list before going into a group activity. These are the behaviours the observers will be looking for and marking you against.

From time to time you will see the observers writing things down. This can feel very similar to a driving test where it is automatically intimidating to see someone so near, noting something down – but please try to relax. They may simply be writing comments such as 'good eye contact' and so it is best to try to ignore all scribblings as much as possible.

After a set period of time, perhaps an hour, the activity will be stopped whether you have made the decision, solved the problem or finished the meeting. The objective from the observer's point of view is to see you in action and they will have seen plenty of you in an hour! At this point you will probably be asked to leave the room to have a break, while the assessors retire to write up their notes and confer.

Put very briefly then, the process is:

1.   You may be given information or a role (if so read thoroughly).

2.   You will be asked to enter the room and sit down.

3.   You will be observed undertaking a group activity and marked on your language, body language, content and style.

4.   You will be stopped after a set amount of time.

5.   You will leave the room.

WHAT TYPES OF GROUP ACTIVITY ARE THERE?

A group activity can literally be any activity that includes a number of people. However they mainly take the form of:

Team meetings

These aim to replicate a typical team meeting. If this is chosen then you will be given an agenda and some notes. You will also need to know what type of team it is and whether there are any issues that need addressing within the meeting.

Important point: these are your team. The assessors will be looking for a team or collaborative approach and therefore you will not receive favour for flaring up or setting yourself (or other team members) against one another or the rest of the team. The days of ruling by fear are long gone in most industries. Also, if you have been given an issue to address (such as excessive sickness), make sure you do and don't skirt around the issue or run out of time.

If you are truly going to manage a team and deliver on your business targets through and with these people they need to look up to you and see leadership at the most and mutual respect at the least. This MUST be exhibited through every part of your communication and that means your actions (even when you think no one is looking). Therefore totally rule out any rolling of the eyes, sarcastic looks, laughing at others contributions, or staring out of the window.

Problem solving groups

This form of group activity will present you with a problem that you are expected to solve. The big mistake that most people make here is that they concentrate on solving the problem – well that is hardly surprising as that is what you are here for isn't it?

Well no actually. If you solve the problem in the allotted time, well and good, but actually you are being assessed on your behavioural skills too. In fact quite often the problem is one that cannot easily be solved and therefore the most you can do is make headway with the group.

Although it is important to work on the problem, what you are being judged on is just HOW you do that.

A good aide memoire for any problem solving situation is to remember the problem solving triangle shown below:

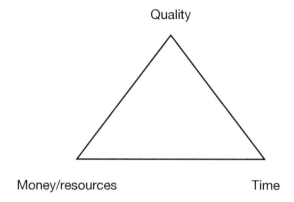

Quality

Money/resources   Time

These factors can be independently manipulated to solve most problems. For example if you are working in a publishing company and are looking of new ways to reduce the cost of publishing a new catalogue of your books, you could look at:

Adjusting the quality – use cheaper paper, include less pictures of covers, reduce the number of pages, or even produce it on line.

Money/resources – could you divert some more money from another project to this to retain the quality, after all this is an income generating project and the shop-front for your business? Do we need to assess how potential loss of sales could correlate to the brochure (for example if every £10 of brochure price nets £50 of sales wouldn't it be worth paying?)

Time – time costs money. Would we save money (that could then be invested) if we were able to reduce the amount of time spent on this project? Would it be cheaper if we actually took longer over the project (you often pay for speed such as in cases of delivery)? How about if the brochures were produced abroad and transported via the cheapest route?

As you can see all areas could be adjusted either up or down and having this picture in your mind will enable you to have something to work to in the meeting and free you up from worrying about something to say, therefore enabling you to concentrate instead on how you interact with everyone.

OK, so you now have that model in your back pocket – how should you approach this exercise?

After the general introductions see if anyone would like to chair the meeting and suggest an appropriate process or structure for the task. If no one comes forward then suggest yourself.

You need to start off by looking at the problem. Why is it a problem? For whom? What impact does this have on the business? Find out how it impacts on each person and their business area by asking everyone to comment on where they see issues with the problem from their own business perspective.

Explore where there are unknowns and assumptions (because this is likely to be a role play exercise) and put those up on flip chart if possible.

Get everyone to contribute towards possible solutions and if you are the chair, steer the discussion. However, if you are not the chair you will need to demonstrate your realms of influence by suggesting a structure or way forward for the meeting.

Therefore:

1. The race is not on to find the quickest solution

2. You must involve everyone in the discussions

3. Work out first how you are going to work together as a group

4. Make a joint plan as to how you use your time in the group (AND the process you will go through)

5. Ensure everyone has a fair chance to speak

6. Note up on a flip chart (if there is one) everyone's ideas (and explore whether there are areas where you lack information or knowledge).

7.   Don't worry if you do not get as far as solving the problem by the end of the meeting.

Decision making groups

Decision making is a natural partner that sits alongside problem solving but is slightly different.

Here the assessors will definitely be looking for a structured approach. It is not sufficient to make an ad hoc decision unless you own the company, and there may very well be a time when you are called to justify your decision to the Board.

So let's get going...

After the general introductions see if anyone would like to chair the meeting and suggest an appropriate process or structure for the task. If no one comes forward then suggest yourself.

Decision making is not simply about coming forward with ideas, it is how you work with the ideas of others and deal with rafts of information. After all, if twelve people sit around the table and just shout out ideas, how is anyone going to manage that information? Whose was the best idea? Well mine of course!! Therefore voting for the best one would not be a good idea as we would all vote for our own.

No, there has to be a structure that is agreed with group as to how you will manage the task, including how you will make the final decision. You may well decide that everyone shouts out ideas, but if so there must be a way of weighting or measuring that information against certain criteria. This is where you will need a decision grid with the best ideas down the side and the criteria across the top. Using this method you will be able to rate your ideas against the criteria. This gives you a logical and justifiable way of making your decision. For example, if you wanted to know which restaurant to book your Christmas luncheon at, try this:

	The Old House	The Roe Buck	Maggie's Kitchen	The Karu House
Must serve vegetarian food	✔	✔	✔	✔
Have a traditional Christmas dinner	✔	✔	✔	✘
Plenty of parking	✘	✔	✘	✔
Must be open from 12.30 until 4.00 pm	✔	✔	✘	✔

You can see from the example above that the only place that you can hold the Christmas luncheon this year (according to the criteria) would be The Roe Buck because it the only choice that satisfies all the criteria.

Grids such as this are used regularly for decision making as they are justifiable and aid the funnelling down and sifting of ideas that is required to come to one final decision. If there are several outcomes that meet the criteria, then you would need to suggest further study. For example if three of the four eating houses above met the criteria, then we need more criteria to enable the final decision. That might mean that another piece of work needs to take place outside of the meeting, and you would be looking for a volunteer from the group to take this forward. Taste testing anyone? Count me in!!

Therefore:

1. The process is to broaden the subject out to collect ideas, and then later narrow it down again towards a decision

2. You must involve everyone and try to make sure everyone contributes

3. Process is vital, and make sure everyone agrees at every juncture

4. Create criteria that everyone is happy with

5. Measure the group's ideas against the criteria

6. Look at your results and suggest a way forward

7. Don't worry if you do not get as far as making the end decision by the end of the meeting – it is fine to suggest further work is needed.

Debating

Holding a debating group activity adds a little extra to the mix. Not only are you demonstrating how you work with others and in a group but you are also demonstrating your values and thought processes. It is almost impossible to debate a subject without giving a lot of yourself away. This can be a good thing or not – depending on your views. For example, if you were to go to an assessment centre at a Pharmaceutical company you may be faced with debating 'Should animals be used for pharmaceutical testing?'

Consider for one moment how you stand on this (highly emotive) subject. It would be impossible to debate this subject without revealing your core values and principles, and the debating itself may get you rather hot under the collar, whichever side of the debate you are on.

Consider also if you were asked to uphold the debate for the other side of the argument. What would you say? Would you be able to deliver? Perhaps you would find that one step too far? Only you can decide but you will be judged on your response.

Debates are often thought in terms of polar opposites but there is usually some common ground that both sides can agree on, and this should be explored and noted. We all have differing views about life's issues and you need not to appear as if an open discussion quickly becomes open combat! Neither is it OK to just have one dogged view, in a debating exercise you must be able to substantiate that view.

Therefore:

1. Think about your values – how do you really feel about this subject?

2. If you are asked to hold a view that is not your own, consider first how this makes you feel. If you can live with it, then go with it.

3. Just because it is a debate does not mean that it is an argument. It needs a structure.

4. Start by asking everyone to share their views.

5. Decide as a group how you are going to include everyone's ideas.

6. Work together to elicit areas of common agreement.

7. Remember you are still being observed – the debate is only the vehicle for a discussion. IT IS STILL A TEAM ACTIVITY.

Negotiating

Negotiating is a high level skill and it takes any form of debating one step higher. A debate may centre on you holding your view but in a negotiation the emphasis is on persuading and influencing the other person to accept your view. For this to happen, finding that common ground on which you can agree can become even more important, for if we can find an area of agreement we can explore our difference from that point.

All managers need to negotiate and in essence all of us need to be able to undertake this skill in varying areas of our lives. For example, have you ever wanted to negotiate on the price of a car? A new house? Some furniture? Your future salary? All of these are real life situations where we need to negotiate. Doing so in a group activity is simply taking that one step further.

A word to the wise: if you are thinking of annihilating your opponent here, you need to think again. You may walk away the winner but that approach is not good for long term business. The other party will feel small and insignificant and will not want to do business with you again. This approach is often called **I win:you lose** and it is not a good outcome in business. Let's look at the other possible outcomes:

I lose:you win – This is great for you as you may now feel on top of the world, feeling that you have won over me, but it is not long until I start feeling resentful. Whether I blame you for winning or myself for being weak and ill prepared, I do not feel like I want to meet with you again. I may even feel that the power ratio between us has shifted in your favour. All in all, once again not a helpful way to continue in business and a situation I would rather forget than be reminded of – and therefore I would not be seeking you out in the future (and I am sure your observer will not think well of you losing to a competitor outright – it does not bode well for the business).

I lose:you lose – Oh dear, what happened here? In this position we both lost. Perhaps neither of us negotiated a good deal, or we failed to reach a settlement – leaving us both feeling frustrated and dissatisfied.

On a positive note, if we recognise the situation in time we could adjourn or re-think our approach – possibly setting another date in the near future to come together again but any assessor observing you here would score you a very low mark.

I win:you win – This is what you should be aiming for, both parties gaining from the negotiation. The outcome may not necessarily benefit both equitably but there are positive outcomes for each. Look at these three separate examples:

I pay a lower price	They have their money in now
I will give up my share on this project	They offer me a different project
I get to save 6 months of living costs and the opportunity to learn another language	They get a manager to take on a foreign project and live abroad for 6 months

In each instance we both give and gain something.

The great thing about getting to Win: Win is that it preserves the relationship. You will have no problems negotiating with this person again and that builds a solid foundation to your future working relationship – and this is why you should be aiming for this outcome.

'Easy,' you might say, 'when there are just two of you but what about eight people in the room?'

Again you (or someone in the group) must find out what people want to get out of the negotiation. There must be some 'non-negotiables' as well as some 'concessions' – tease out these to find out where commonalities can be accommodated easily. Also try to ascertain links. For example if there is only a small pot of money and you all want to undertake training programmes, do any of the projects link in any way? Can you share the money by sharing the training? Finally think about creative solutions. What could you get for free? The room? The trainer? Lunch? Can any of it be provided in a different format? Webinars? E-learning? All of these would bring down the cost of the training programme.

Focus on:

- Commonalities
- Links
- Creative solutions

Whilst all the time working WITH the group.

Therefore:

1. You are still in a group activity. Whatever the solution, it has to be agreed by THE GROUP.

2. Ensure everyone outlines their situation so that all the information is in the room.

3. At this point you could rate them as 'non-negotiable' and 'negotiable' if you want to write up notes.

4. Try to find those links (a clue here is that they are usually more evident in role play than in real life).

5. Work with the group to find a number of creative solutions so that everyone is helping each other with their topic/issue.

6. Re-cap the outcomes and also remember to keep involving everyone in the group to ensure they are happy with the progress.

7. For **win:win** to be an outcome, every member of the group should walk away with something even if it is not exactly what they wanted at the beginning.

CONSENSUS AND INFLUENCING

In certain industries you may be asked to work by consensus. This usually means that everyone must agree at every step before the group can move onto the next step. The philosophy underpinning consensus is that because everyone agrees at each stage there is a joint responsibility for the outcome and no one can say that they did not agree at a later date.

This approach means that where there is disagreement, it has to be dealt with at that moment, otherwise the process cannot move forward. This can sometimes put pressure on the individual to agree just to move on, which of course then makes a nonsense of the consensus. People should not be either bored or pressed into submission. Therefore if you are asked to work this way, you need to consider how you will influence and interact with any member of the group who is preventing the groups progress to the next stage.

When achieved consensus creates very sound outcome but it can slow down the process.

LET'S LOOK AT AN EXAMPLE OF A GROUP ACTIVITY

Here is a very simple one:

You are part of the South East Training Group and the group has just been awarded £25,000 in a grant to pay for some training that furthers your organisation.

Each of you has been away and undertaken some background research and you are now coming together to decide how you will spend the money. There are six organisations that make up this group and each of you is a representative of that organisation and has been given a card outlining your own situation.

As a group decide on the outcome.

THE CARDS

South East Volunteers

You work for South East Volunteers, a voluntary group who offer a range of skills to those in need. Volunteers can undertake any activity from painting a wall or tidying a garden, to sitting with someone for an hour or simply peeling some potatoes. Everyone who volunteers has to have a security check and an induction (including health and safety, manual handling training). These volunteers save the country thousands of pounds and bring pleasure to many. Unfortunately your finance director has 'emigrated' with the money and you are now in dire straits if your company is to continue. You need £7,000 to train a new team just to survive.

South East Environmentalist Group

You work for South East Environmentalist Group, a team of highly organised individuals focussed on saving the environment. You have run highly prized campaigns in awareness, but you now need one member of the team to undertake a huge study of the Environmental Impact in the Urban Community. A local university has said that they can part fund this and therefore you only need £5,000 – and at the end of it you will have national prominence AND a member of staff with a highly prized professional qualification. The outcomes could be amazing for urban populations in the future.

Healthcare in the Community

You work for Healthcare in the Community and you support carers who care for others at home. This is a growing market and therefore you need to secure substantial funding to run training programmes to ensure your carers are well trained in health and safety, feeding and administering medicines. The amount you are looking for is £10,000 (but there is the opportunity of trying for some other funding in six month's time if you are unsuccessful).

Childmind

You work for Childmind a support group for parents of children with learning difficulties. Childmind is a funded group but their future is in doubt and the funding does not include training anyway. If they can be self supporting, there may be a future for the group and therefore you want to ask for £5,000 to run a campaign and a number of creativity sessions for fund raising and (if the money stretches) perhaps some money towards getting their ideas off the ground.

The Immunisation Team

You work for the Immunisation Team, a funded team who aim to provide information and vaccines for immunising people in difficult to reach communities. Their client group would not go to their GP for many reasons, and this is why the team was created. You would like £10,000 to run a complete campaign raising awareness and offering flu vaccines in the first instance. Research has told you that if people come forward for the flu vaccine, they can then be persuaded to undertake further vaccination

Remember – you have seen all the cards but in a real group activity you would not see anyone's but your own. How would you begin to deal with this in a team activity situation?

Write some notes here:

Check if your ideas are similar to mine.

OK, these are not a blueprint for success but my thoughts here would be:

1. Welcome everyone to the group and reiterate why we are here today.

2. Add any 'rules' about the meeting such as when it must finish and whether another is possible.

3. Ask everyone to introduce themselves, say a little about their organisation and what they are hoping for today.

4. As a rough guide add up the total amount of requests to see whether it is possible to accommodate everyone within the pot of money.

5. Open the meeting to the group for an open discussion and invite bids for their project.

6. At all times be looking for links and commonalities that can be introduced into the group (it is often amazing that others cannot see them even if they seem obvious).

7. Be creative – look for where reductions can be made, can the project be run next year? Over two financial years to split the cost? Are there any economies that could be made? Ask each person directly to consider this in light of their own project. As you have not seen their card it might surprise you what they come up with.

8. Keep a check on the time and two-thirds of the way through the meeting, start to try to move toward an agreement as this could take some time.

9. Don't forget to influence and persuade others to accept ideas and/or work together.

10. If possible, within the time frame, come to some form of conclusion. Write it up and check with everyone that they agree.

Now let's look at what the observers are looking for:

Exercise 1 – some pre-work, before the assessment centre.

Look at the five principles in the BabyMaxPro case study at the back of this book.

If you were being observed what behaviours would you expect to see and hear, as an observer, in a group activity. Note them below:

Principle	Behaviour in the meeting
Focus on the customer	
Respect for everyone	
Innovation	
Collaboration	
Commercial awareness	

How did you get on? Did you also read the information printed in the paragraphs below the Principles?

Compare your ideas with some of mine below:

Principle	Behaviour in the meeting
Focus on the customer	Demonstrating a consideration for others
	Keeping BabymaxPro's core products at the forefront of your discussions
	If any of the other people involved in the group are actually playing your customer, a full appreciation of their work with your company
	Demonstrating that you are listening effectively and taking their comments seriously
Respect for everyone	Showing due care and involving everyone in the room
	Not cutting across or talking down to others
	Actively listening and empathising with others
	Not pulling rank or forcefully becoming the manager
	Being inclusive rather than autocratic
Innovation	Showing due care and involving everyone in the room
	Not cutting across or talking down to others
	Actively listening and empathising with others
	Not pulling rank or forcefully becoming the manager
	Being inclusive rather than autocratic

Collaboration	Being inclusive with the group
	Taking on your own fair share of the work
	Suggesting grouping together
	Noticing links and areas for joint work
	Good eye contact and body language
Commercial awareness	Demonstrating that you understand the business issues
	Demonstrating knowledge of the outside business environment
	Knowing which are your core or strong products and protecting them
	Appreciating the wider business market (professional collaborations, foreign markets etc)

Exercise 2 – the team exercise

Read back through the BabyMaxPro Case Study

You are Helen Maxwell the Director and you have three other people in the meeting with you, Phil Read, Chris Bright and Mary Stevens. They have both just come back into the office and want to discuss their emails with you. You need to find a collaborative way forward that ties in with BabyMaxPro's direction and strategy in addition to their values.

Make notes here about what process you need to follow, as the Director/ Owner you will be expected to lead:

What do you need to consider in each instance?

Some ideas are shown over page.

These are just some of my ideas, and you may have had others:

The process

Helen will need to keep a managing arm on the meeting process.

Although she wouldn't do introductions she may want to set some guidelines for working.

Helen will want to see results as her time is precious. She will want to give clear direction. She must make sure that whatever goes forward MUST be in the best interest of BabyMaxPro for the future. There is a need to return to original values (as shown in the Vision) and she needs to manage everyone's expectations of what can be achieved.

Do not be seduced into thinking that some of the items are less important or shorter than others – they are all of equal importance to the business.

Considerations

Phil Read: Phil believes that he has stumbled on a small project that, if he does not snap it up, someone else will discover. He believes this to be unique but has not yet done any research into whether this is true (and even whether they could deliver in the quantities that BabyMaxPro would expect). Helen needs to be careful about introducing new products into an already straining workforce. She has to remember the failure of the BabyMaxPro clothing label and consider how and why this might be different. She also needs to consider whether it is indeed clothing and if not, where it would sit in her company.

Chris Bright: Chris has seen another product that might interest BabyMaxPro. It is already being exhibited and therefore is already in production. There is also concern that another product is being marketed as frighteningly similar to BabyMaxPro cream. This needs immediate investigation as it could be breaking the law or at least significantly dent BabyMaxPro profits – especially if it is being sold cheaper and gaining market share.

Mary Stevens: Mary is asking for a decision on some training. She wants a bespoke programme that addresses some of the issues raised in the Annual Colleague Survey. Is it urgent? That is for Helen to decide, but Mary wants to bring the consultant's in. Is this the right time? There is a danger of being too hasty.

CHAPTER 6
PRESENTATIONS

Do presentations make you feel nervous? If you have that sinking feeling then don't despair. For assessment centre presentations you need to feel sufficiently anxious to create immediacy and a little frisson but not so nervous that you become debilitated by the process.

There are two aspects we need to look at here:

1. Your material

2. You!

YOUR MATERIAL

Let's start with your material. You will find that when you have your material in order and organised then you will find that you are more than halfway there. Being organised and knowing the points you want to get across will give you confidence, which will go a long way to helping you when you are facing your assessors.

First of all it helps to be familiar with the situation. You will probably be asked to present to a group of around 2-6 people who will most probably be sitting in front of you.

You do not have to stand but it can look too casual if you sit (and of course there may not be a chair set out for you) – in which case, plan on standing, and then if you are invited to sit, you can.

You should be told in advance the equipment that will be at your disposal. If you are not given this information, try to contact personnel beforehand to check. It could throw you completely if you turn up with a set of slides only to find there is no equipment in the room. (Many years ago I turned up with a presentation only to find that it did not play on the company's software. I did eventually manage to get it sorted but by then was 20 mins late and had involved the entire IT department – not a great way to start)!

There is no problem with using a flip chart (if so, take your own pens) or simply standing and delivering your presentation, with heart, and no materials or technology at all. The important point is that you feel comfortable and your presentation represents you, for example if you were presenting to motivate sales professionals a set of cold slides would achieve less than a more personal rousing motivational call to action.

To conclude, use the materials that suits both your style and the subject matter. For example, if you want to convey a complex notion or figure comparison, it helps to have that pictorially as a diagram or chart. However, if the job involved sales and you are telling me what a great product this is, you may not need slides at all, and prefer to use your personal charm and personality to get your message across.

Important point: – think about what you are attempting to convey. How complex is the material? How much do you want them to see your personality shining through? How important is it that you are personally convincing?

Finally you will be told when to start and you should have been given a guide as to how long you are expected to speak for. Between five and twenty minutes is usual. This gives you long enough to structure a presentation and represent yourself but not so long that the panel are there all day.

The assessment panel will be timing you and therefore it is ESSENTIAL that you are able to keep to that time. Presentations are a key part of management and the ability to keep to time is a skill that demonstrates personal control. Overrun and you may have points deducted from your performance, and you cannot afford to make silly mistakes like that.

Structuring material

Even if you are not going to produce slides, it helps to think in terms of slides (or cue cards) as they are easy to remember and give you structure. Whether you then use them or not will depend on you and your delivery style.

Having a clear structure is hugely important. It will:

- enable you to provide a cohesive argument
- enable your audience or panel to follow through your points
- provide you with an easy 'roadmap' to follow, should you drift off course or lose confidence.

Your presentation needs to be balanced and even in content and therefore it helps to separate it out into chunks. A rule of thumb is that each slide should carry only basic information and allow for 2-3 minutes of speaking time, at which point the presenter can discuss the points made on the slide. In addition there will be an introduction slide and an end slide.

Let's illustrate this as an example. Imagine you have been asked to produce a 15 minute presentation on 'Green issues in the office environment.'

This information helps us to calculate that for a 15 minute presentation we need:

One introductory slide that has a title or heading and our name

No more than 5 slides for the main part of our talk (at just under 3 minutes each)

One final slide that either says 'Any questions?' or 'Thank you'

Now that you know you only have five slides to get your point across in main section of the presentation, you will need to make each slide work hard within a structure or argument. Therefore we could pull together:

Our introductory slide – the title of my presentation together with my name

Slide 1 – why offices need to consider green issues with a list of points

Slide 2 – where considering green issues can have an impact on the environment and business

Slide 3 – a list of easy ways that can incorporate green issues into office life, for example, recycling

Slide 4 – a list of benefits to staff and the business

Slide 5 – what you intend to (or the business could) do about it – actions

Final slide – summary and a call for any questions.

Important point – do not cram information onto your slide or paper. Try to have no more than five bullet points on each slide, under the heading, and if you need to show something complex such as a spreadsheet, build in time allocation for your audience to read it.

That example was very lightweight. There is insufficient time in 15 minutes to delve into why people do or don't do things (analysis of their behaviour) or to discuss the future of the world – and so if time is at a premium keep it short, light, and snappy. The old adage of three parts – "Tell 'em what you are going to tell 'em, tell 'em, and then tell 'em what you told 'em" is so true. Like every good story it should have a great start and a completely satisfying end, leaving the panel feeling that you have not sold them short. You have delivered exactly what they asked for and have not overrun, in a neat little presentation that has structure, but has also allowed you to present your views and demonstrate your personality – perfect!

Now you have a very quick go, using the method above. Imagine I asked you to come up with a very general 15 minute presentation on 'The future for staff development in your organisation.' Have a go at structuring some slides with just your initial thoughts on the next page.

Introductory slide:

Slide 1

Slide 2

Slide 3

Slide 4

Slide 5

Summary slide

How did you get on? You could have put anything as there is no right answer, but I have given an example here just in case you were stuck:

Introductory slide:

The future for staff development in our organisation

my name

Slide 1

Perhaps a quote about learning or a definition of what development means

Slide 2

Some points regarding what we do to develop staff at the moment

(and maybe some statistics?)

Slide 3

What is the trend in the 'wider world' at the present time

Slide 4

The benefits of incorporating some of the ideas of others

Slide 5

What this actually means we have to do – action points

Summary slide

Thank you

Any questions?

Notice how I bring it to action at the end again? Philosophising is all very well but some good strong action points will serve you well and may get you more marks. (Note that if you don't include HOW you are going to do something, consider it anyway as you may be asked at the end of your presentation). It is too easy to say, 'We must change the culture' without saying actually how you intend to achieve that, and you would not want to be put on the spot without an answer.

Quick tip: most of the presentation topics or questions you will be asked to present will be a) asking you to look into the future, and b) what you would do? For example: If you were the manager of the new team, what would be your strategy and your first priority actions? Or 'If you were fortunate to secure the job, what changes would you make to the culture and how?

Powerpoint presentations

A few quick pointers if you decide to go with powerpoint or any of the other presentation tools available.

- Check that the software you are using is compatible with that of the company

- Decide how you are going to take your presentation, on a device or a digital USB stick (and clear that with the company as not every organisation will allow you to link up their computers to external drives)

- Turn off any music and use the minimum of animation – although entertaining for a large function, it is distracting in this situation. The panel want to hear you and will not want to be waylaid by technology.

- Hold back on using too many colours or fonts. Colour can be unpredictable on the screen and you simply want a good clean font for business use. Use a large font size so that your message is clear and fills the screen.

- Ensure you can move from slide to slide with ease (and know how to go backwards through the slides too)

Just to recap:

1. Identify a simple structure

2. Carve your main message into sections (or slides)

3. Do not have too many slides – 2-3 minutes of speaking per slide

4. Do not overload your slides – try to resist more than five bullet points

5. Check, check and check again for spelling mistakes

6. Use a header and tail slide so that you announce the presentation at the beginning and it does not suddenly finish without a suitable ending

7. If you prefer to use other methods of presenting and feel they more reflect you and the situation – then do so

YOU

I said there was another part to this and here we are… I want to talk about you and how you will actually present. Now I know that nerves can overcome the best of people, but for this presentation you need to be sure that you are going to convey the information you have designed to the best of your ability.

The image and mood you want to convey is that of professional competence. This does not mean that you cannot deliver a light-hearted speech but it must be appropriate to the situation and be natural – therefore no contrived jokes!

You should now be clear about your material and that should give you some confidence and so, draw yourself up to your full height and ensure that your head is looking forward and nicely balanced, not up at the sky or down at your feet.

If you are presenting from a standing position, stand with your feet slightly apart, to give you a good solid base and keep your hands at your sides or clasped in front of you. If it helps you can carry notes but not a script. Keep a note to hand of any important facts you want to be sure to convey or any tricky names (that seem to evade everyone at the key moment), or figures that you need to be absolutely accurate. Either keep this note in your hand or put it where you can easily glance at it in an emergency.

Stand to the side of the screen (if you have one) and position yourself so that you can turn your head just a little to see the bullet points on the screen, but not so that you are tempted to read the screen. The audience can read the screen for themselves, and do not need to be told what is up there, your job is to 'put some flesh on those bones' with your description of the key words. Talk around the bullet points, but engage and speak with your audience – again not at the screen. It is very tempting to fix your eyes on the screen but it will alienate your audience if you do so for any length of time.

Nerves

As I mentioned at the beginning of this chapter, if you were not nervous or at least a little apprehensive, I would worry about that. Some nerves are totally understandable and acceptable but what can you do to stop them running away with you altogether?

Remember to keep breathing! I know this may sound odd but when we get nervous we take in less oxygen and breathe at a faster and more shallow rate. This does not deliver sufficient oxygen to where it is needed and we begin to feel light headed and anxious. Our main reaction is to try to access more oxygen by breathing faster but actually what we should be doing is taking in deeper breaths. Therefore slow your breathing down and take deeper, more meaningful breaths (this will also slow your speech down, which is helpful as we tend to speak faster when we are tense).

If you have the tendency to shake, then stand firm. Imagine that you are a tree with roots that go down into the ground and feel rooted to the spot. Sit down if you prefer and try to resist bringing attention to your nervousness as it is very possible that no one has noticed.

Eye contact

It is as simple as this – look at your audience and speak TO them, not AT them. In a business setting these people will be your future team and you will have a good rapport with them – remember it is only for today that it may feel awkward.

Smile and look directly at everyone as you speak in the same way as you would if you were speaking to your family or colleagues. Engaging everyone is important and that is something you can do by simply looking into their eyes.

... and finally

Try to be yourself. I know this sounds corny but each of us has a presenting style that is natural to us. Unless you have had feedback in the past that you need to change your style – accept how you present and see it as an extension of your style.

The panel do not want to see a load of clones and there is something satisfying in noting that someone has a unique style that defines them, and further that they can use that style to reach out to the audience.

Just to recap:

1. Be prepared with all your notes in order.

2. Take deep breaths (without gasping) to lower your anxiety.

3. Smile and make good eye contact with your assessors before starting. This will set a good tone for your presentation.

4. Do not try to stifle your natural style.

5. If you are standing, make sure you have a solid base.

6. Keep any important notes to hand and one eye on the clock.

7. Present with confidence, knowing that your material is good and that you have prepared well.

MEDIA PRESENTATIONS

For some positions the ability to speak to the media is an intrinsic part of the job. This could involve how you deliver set statements on behalf of the organisation or a full interview. If this particular skill is required then it is likely that it will form part of the assessment centre content. This would involve you being interviewed either by someone playing a news journalist or interviewer whilst being filmed.

This will put you under immediate pressure but will also provide the assessors with material they can review later, and therefore your performance will be replayed at a later time, when the assessors confer.

As a rule of thumb, never accept blame either yourself or on behalf of your organisation, and practice using some deflecting techniques. However, if you are applying for a role that includes significant media possibilities, you need to consider how you react under pressure and practice as much beforehand as possible. Many medial companies have training programmes for help with this particular skill and it may be worth investing if you feel that your future career lies in your ability to handle the media effectively.

ONE FINAL IMPORTANT POINT!

Before we leave this subject and move into our final exercise there is one aspect of the presentation that I have not covered – your opinion. Yes, the panel are there to assess your presentation style, and yes, they will be looking at your content and organisation of data – but there is one final aspect that only you alone can bring to the presentation – your views.

If the presentation topic asks you to determine a future for part of the company, or whether you think the company should do a or b, they are asking for your opinion – what you would do in that situation. This is a tricky one as there is no right or wrong answer, and of course you cannot know what the company is planning or whether the situation is real or not. My advice here is to go with the option you believe to be in the best interests of the company but make sure you justify why you think that is the correct path to take – after all you would have to justify your decisions to shareholders. However, your views are important, and more so in some instances. I can remember once being asked for my views on animal testing by a pharmaceutical company. Be prepared to be tested on your views as well as the presentation.

EXERCISE

Read back through the BabbyMaxPro case study at the end of this book and then design a 15 minute presentation on the following:

How the BabyMaxPro Principles can help the company deliver their vision for the future. You have 30 minutes to design your presentation.

OK, how did you get on?

Obviously I could not see your presentation or delivery style but this is a very typical question – one where you are asked to take material given to you earlier and tie it together with an added dash of your own thoughts for the future.

You could have answered this in any way that you wanted but the most obvious way is to use the five principles as your five main slides. This would have given you:

An introductory slide with the title and your name

Slide 1 – Commercial awareness

Slide 2 – Collaboration

Slide 3 – Innovation

Slide 4 – Respect for everyone

Slide 5 – Focus on the customer

Summary slide – either tying all the points together or a 'Thank you' message

This would break down nicely into allowing 2-3 minutes per slide, which could then each carry up to five bullet points that you could discuss as part of your presentation.

If you had time and the resources available you could provide handouts for the panel, or you could offer to send through the presentation slides electronically, thereby also demonstrating that you understood about working in paperless systems.

Naturally this is only one interpretation of the task and you may have attempted it entirely differently. Neither one is right or wrong and I am sure you could win me over to your ideas through your persuasive presentation!!

CHAPTER 7
THE WRITTEN REPORT

It is expected in any role of management that you are able to construct a cohesive management report. Used as part of an assessment centre the written report allows assessors to assess your:

- Writing skills – how you write, your style, tone and even the clarity of your handwriting (most assessment centres will not provide you with a computer)
- Communication skills – how you convey ideas and complex situations, and how you express and sell ideas
- Ideas and problem solving – how you are able to assimilate information and arrive at workable solutions
- Assumptions – the assumptions you make (and need to make) around the information you are given, generating ideas and any possible solutions.

Quite a lot then! Which is why the written report is a popular choice for assessment centres, it reveals so much about you, your style and the way you lead staff.

BASIC REPORT WRITING

A report, as opposed to an essay, is a well organised, systematic document that analyses a situation or problem, provides a discussion or evaluation of the facts, and then usually concludes with a recommendation. Clarity is crucial as is clear and unambiguous language, and finally it must be written in an appropriate way for the situation and audience. For example you would not write to your Boss in the same way that you would to your friend.

A full-blown report would have a set structure that is similar to:

- A title page
- Any acknowledgements
- Terms of reference (or a definition of the task, so that your remit is clear to the reader)
- Executive summary (if included – this is a short one page version of the whole report to provide an overview)
- Method used or a procedure
- Main body or findings
- Detailed discussion
- Summary
- Conclusion/Recommendations
- Appendices
- References (if any)
- Bibliography

Phew!! That is rather a lot to write in an hour – which is why your management report will be a much shorter report featuring simply:

- An introduction (including the problem as you interpret it)
- The main points to note
- A discussion including your ideas
- A conclusion with your recommendation.

Now that is more achievable in one hour, isn't it?

ADDING A MODEL TO GIVE YOU STRUCTURE

In the same way that your presentation benefits from structure, so too does your report, if you are not to produce some rambling diatribe!

Some people are essayists by nature and a structure comes easily to them, but for others it is important to create a way of ensuring every aspect is covered in the shortest possible time. If you (like me) are in the second category, here are two really useful and easy ways of ensuring you cover everything.

As throughout this book, I will demonstrate the two techniques to you through examples, and then you can see which one is most comfortable for you and would be the most appropriate for use in the example you have been given.

The example assessment assignment we are going to use for this is:

Helen has asked you to write a report (including recommendations) for integrating a leadership training programme into the company.

TECHNIQUE #1 – USING MINDMAPPING™

Mindmapping™ is the invention of Tony Buzan who has written countless books on the subject. His technique is to use mind association to capture ideas by mimicking the workings of the brain. His books are great and show this technique in depth but for now we are just going to demonstrate the principles through grouping common ideas.

At the end of this section you will see what appears to be a blank page with a central section. This is a map that has been started for you by placing the idea or nub of the report in the centre.

From this you are going to draw 'arms' (like an octopus) similar to the one shown, and place an idea that occurs to you on each 'tentacle'. (As in my example below).

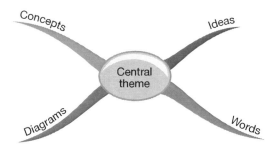

Now from those initial 'tentacles' draw off other 'filaments' with other related ideas that you feel should be included in this section. Keep going, adding more tentacles if needed, until you feel that you have sufficiently captured your ideas and the diagram is complete.

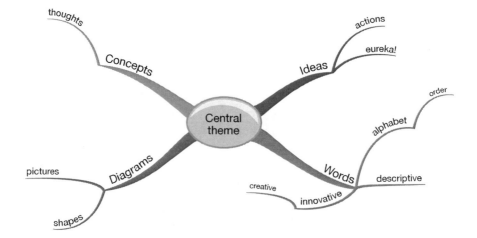

From this central section draw on your own 'tentacle' and 'filaments'
pertaining to Leadership in BabyMaxPro...

You could have gone in any direction you wanted but, as in all my other examples throughout this book, I have provided you with an example of my thoughts below:

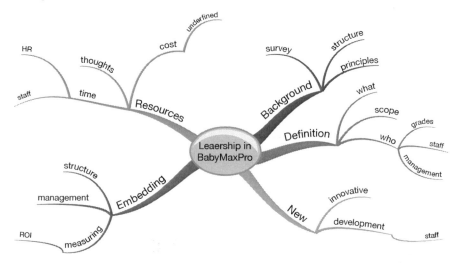

Now start to link ideas and issues together by drawing dotted lines, and note any duplicated ideas. Finally decide on a natural order for writing your report by putting a 1, 2, 3 etc by each 'tentacle.' You will notice that you now have a natural grouping for each of your paragraphs or headings and, if you follow your numbering system, you can now sit down and write.

This whole process will take you no more than five minutes out of your time and will provide you with a cohesively structured report that covers every aspect – just leaving you to consider your recommendation!!

TECHNIQUE #2 – USING A MODEL

Another technique is to use a well known model to ensure you cover all ground and provide a rounded and full answer.

There are many management models available but the one I would recommend you consider for this exercise is the McKinsey 7 S model. It is simply:

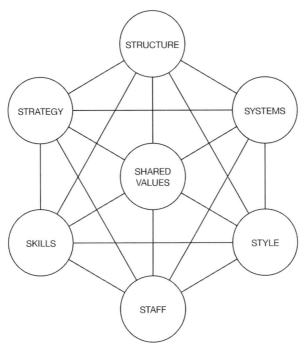

McKinsey's 7 S model

This model simply represents all the factors that need to be considered when thinking through a change situation and introducing a leadership programme is a change.

Using this model as an aide memoir we can begin to think through the issues for each part of the model. Take a moment to make a note on the following pages what you think the issues might be for introducing leadership training programme into BabyMaxPro in each section.

Structure

Systems

Style

Staff

Skills

Strategy

Shared Values

Using these as headings is very similar to placing them along the 'tentacles' of a Mindmap™ – but in an easy to remember, linear way.

Again, you will have your own ideas and interpretations but here are some considerations that I thought you might need to discuss in your report:

Structure

The company has grown organically. Is the structure in the right shape for introducing leadership?

Is the HR 'department' large enough to cope with running this programme?

Who would be included in the leadership programme (certain people, above a particular grade, management, or everyone)?

Systems

How you envisage the system of leadership (both the actual leadership and the logistics of the training) would take place and work.

How you would keep track of everyone's development. Will you use a computerised system?

How to publicise and market the new programme both internally (to staff) and externally in the press.

Style

How might this programme influence the style of BabyMaxPro and in what way?

How would the programme fit with helping to achieve the vision for the company?

Who will need to model the new behaviours and how will they be measured?

Staff

What impact this will have on staff (those present and future employees)?

What will be the return on investment (ROI) and how will you measure that?

How do believe staff will be affected by the new programme?

Skills

How will this programme equip staff to take BabyMaxPro into the future?

What skills can they hope to acquire?

What is in it for them?

How will BabyMaxPro maintain and further develop these new skills?

Strategy

How this programme will fit with all our other work and the future direction of BabymaxPro.

How the leadership programme will create a stronger, better future for BabymaxPro.

What are you trying to achieve through this programme and how real is that?

Shared Values

Is everyone 'on board' with this programme (including shareholders)?

How you can ensure that the finished programme delivers on the shared company values.

Can you see that by using the model you cover all bases of your discussion? Following on from a short introduction around leadership and how valuable it is in the current working environment, you can then dedicate a paragraph to each of these topics thereby ensuring that you have discussed the entire subject from almost every angle, before moving in towards your final conclusion and recommendation.

I cannot write the business report for you, and you will have your very own style, but I am sure that given these prompts and the fact that in the real world you are actually interested in going for the particular job on offer, you would be able to construct a reasonable report that considers all possibilities for the chosen topic.

Tip: you will be assessed on content as well as style, grammar and punctuation, and therefore you can collect a lot of points by demonstrating that you can analyse the situation fully, even if you fall foul of a few misspellings.

It does not matter which of the two techniques you choose (or even if you use both), the most important aspect is that you are not floored by the case study you are given. You will have a great deal of your own experience to bring to the report too, and you can weave that throughout your prose.

Now, let's once again use the BabyMaxPro case study at the back of this book and set you a further exercise.

EXERCISE

You are an organisational development consultant brought in to advise BabyMaxPro by Helen and Shaun Maxwell following the results of the Annual Colleague Survey. Write a business report on the outcome of that survey and how you believe it should be taken forward.

Plan in the space below and then two further pages have been left blank for you to write your report.

How did you get on? Did you use a visual Mindmap™, a linear 7 S diagram, a mixture of the two or something completely different?

If you are preparing for an up and coming assessment centre, give your report to a trusted colleague to read through and (hopefully) comment truthfully on your style. However, concerning this exercise, there are some key issues raised in the case study that should be in your report and these are:

- The fact that the business is a family business that has grown organically and therefore the structure possibly needs revisiting to test its appropriateness for the future. There is significant emotional attachment to the company by its founders and it is therefore timely to take an analytical look at the business.

- Although the original BabyMaxPro Cream is still a market leader, it was highly innovative at the time. There are now other similar products entering the marketplace, and therefore it is essential to look at the costs of the business in relation to the profits. This will ensure a robust business even if other manufacturers/businesses encroach on the current market share (you may want to mention that the change in laboratories offers an opportunity to look afresh at any contractual requirements, costs, and so forth).

- The company may have felt a 'wobble' due to what it perceives as a costly mistake in 2004, when in fact this experience helped BabyMaxPro learn some important business lessons. Up until that point they had been effortlessly successful but this is a rare experience in business. Their 'mistake' is only what many businesses experience when they try out a new market, and they must not let it hold them back from future ideas and ventures.

- It is very unusual to have a 100% response rate to a questionnaire – that is to be applauded and demonstrates that the staff are engaged and feel comfortable giving feedback.

- There has been some movement in the survey results of this year, some up and some down.

- The survey results indicate that there is quite a significant reduction in staff feeling happy in their job (compared to last year) – further that they do not feel listened to and feel that there is a communication issue between colleagues and their manager. (You will need to make assumptions as you why you feel that may be the case.)

- There is an increase in staff understanding their role but also an increase in staff bored in their roles. Is the structure too rigid? Has the entrepreneurial element gone out of their jobs? Are staff clear in their actions but limited in scope? Is the current structure of the teams too restrictive?

- The amount of perceived leadership received from managers has dipped – why could this be? Could leadership training be the answer, or is it that staff now understand what leadership is and realise that it is not as evident as they originally thought?

- There is a huge pride and willingness to be a part of BabyMaxPro which indicates a strong and positive staff group (you can link this to their principles). You see a great future for this business.

These are just a few of the points that you may have picked out of the general information and the survey. Now what are you going to suggest?

This is very much up to you as an experienced manager. As you have progressed thus far to an assessment centre it would be assumed that you have experience and knowledge that you can bring to this situation. If you are lost at this point, go back to the 7S model and ask yourself what you could suggest as an action in each of these bulleted points.

Assessors marking management reports are usually looking for a mix of new ideas whilst retaining the traditional values. It would be quite alarming if you suggested changing everything, after all people traditionally don't like change – unless of course the question asks you to completely re-design the business. Therefore I would suggest that you attempt to maintain the overall family feel of the business (as staff seem to want this and it has worked well) but consider and discuss updating certain aspects around structure, increased growth, innovation, and staff development – to name a few!!

CHAPTER 8
THE INTERVIEW

Interviews can be daunting at the best of times. Just when you think that you have been assessed from every angle you are called in to either a one-to-one or to face a panel to answer even more questions. You would be excused for feeling a little under fire and subject to a barrage of questions, and therefore it can be helpful to organise your thought processes before the interview begins to ensure that you gain maximum benefit from the situation.

The overall aim of the interview is two-fold. Yes it is to verify some of the observations and information you have provided throughout the assessment centre, but (and this is a really big BUT) it is also about you having an opportunity to find out whether you think that you will fit into this organisation. In other words it is a two-way conversation to enable you both to perform AND find out more about the organisation and how they tick. If you think of it thus, you will also feel so much less pressured and you will not come across as desperate or needy. Every so often you will meet a company that is very glossy on the outside, but you have the feeling that maybe you would not feel comfortable working there. Perhaps it is the way you are treated throughout the assessment centre for maybe it is a conversation with a member of staff. Unfortunately it happens, and if that is the case, it is better to find out now rather than once you have taken the job.

SINGLE PERSON OR PANEL INTERVIEWS?

As mentioned above the interview may be with just one person or a panel. If it is with one person it is likely that the person undertaking the interview will be the future manager of that role. If that is the case then they will be attempting to verify the centre findings and find out a little bit more about you, the experience you have (which may not have been evidenced through the assessment centre), and how you might fit into the team. If you face a panel interview it is likely that each person on the panel will have their own agenda and perspective. This can make the interview a little more tricky as you are attempting to appeal a range of people, each seeking their own view of an ideal candidate. On a panel interview you may be faced with:

- The team manager (to ascertain that you fit the team and have the right experience)
- The departmental manager (possibly looking at the over-arching array of staff that are needed)
- Possibly an expert in your area of specialism (if you are specialist in one area then you may be need to be questioned at a technical or professional level)
- Someone from personnel (usually to ensure fair play and to answer any questions about terms and conditions of employment)
- Possibly a director/shareholder/politician (to question your views and/ or values)
- A lay person (a member of the public or user of the service) – often used to give an external perspective – very popular in local government interviews.

(You will not have all of these people on a panel, but a selection depending on the position for which you are applying.)

If your interview is a panel interview it is traditional for each person to question you in turn, rather than expect you to field questions from all of them in a hotch, potch manner. This can help as you will then automatically be able to spend some time focussing on the needs of each interviewer in turn.

Important point – it is important at this point to note that although interviews should be about mutual discovery, there may be some pressure added. If you are applying for a job in management or above it would be expected that you will be able to cope with a certain amount of pressure – and firing questions at you is a great way of testing that!

WHAT IS THE INTERVIEW LOOKING FOR?

The interview is there to verify and confirm both your original application and your assessment results. In your original application you will have made various claims to qualifications, knowledge and experience. At this stage your employer may not have any other form of verification as certificate checking and references are traditionally requested at the end, as part of the final administration process for the person who is offered the job. (In some instances they will be requested in advance of the assessment centre, but usually there is little point in requesting over 20 references when there is only one job on offer). If the organisation has no other verification, then assessment staff must achieve that by questioning you and forming judgements based on your answers.

A further point is that the assessment centre is built around the competences required to fulfil the job and work for the organisation. This does not always allow you to put forward other prior experience that you may feel is relevant. For example the assessment centre may cover many things but does not have an activity based on giving difficult feedback to a member of staff. You might be particularly good at this and found that in your previous job you were very successful in this area. How do you get that message across if it has not been extracted through the assessment process? Through the interview of course, because it allows you ample time to push forward your other experience. Another example is that you may have worked in a different industry, say the fashion industry and now you are applying for a job in the engineering industry. It is unlikely that the staff interviewing you will have detailed knowledge of working in the fashion industry and may not see the value of the skills you bring. You need the interview to get your point across, not only proving transferrable skills but also (maybe) some skills that you have, but perhaps they had not thought of as being useful.

Therefore you are looking to:

1. Answer the interviewer's questions to verify your skills, knowledge and experience, and to validate their observations.

2. Propose any new areas of expertise that you feel is relevant to the position.

3. Ask questions about the new position and company.

They are looking for:

1. Explanations of behaviours they may have witnessed or seeking evidence of behaviours that may have been lacking.

2. A comprehensive sales job – why should they chose you?

3. Interest shown in the position on offer and a good discussion.

A note for those facing an assessment centre as part of reorganisation. Having been involved in several of these, one of the biggest traps that applicants fall into is that, at interview, they put forward what they do now and not what they would do in the new job on offer. This is perceived as the applicant not having done their homework around the job to find out what is involved or demonstrating why they are the most suited to the role. This is probably because traditionally an employee would put themselves in the hands of their managers and trust them to slot them into whatever post was suitable – but not now! It is important that you fight for your job and demonstrate that you have spent time thinking about how you will work in the new structure. In most reorganisations there are fewer jobs than staff and therefore if you want to be one of the lucky ones who secure a post, you will have to pull out the stops to show your enthusiasm.

WHAT QUESTIONS WILL THEY ASK?

In the first instance this will largely depend on whether this is an external post you are being interviewed for, or an internal post/reorganisation. If it is an internal post/reorganisation the interviewer(s) are likely to know you and some of your background. They may know where you have worked and what you have done, and this means that they will not be going over this ground again. They are more likely to cut to the chase and move straight into questions concerning the new job.

If this is a new company and you do not know the interviewer(s) then it is more likely that they will begin with a roundup of your career so far. Therefore expect questions such as:

Can you tell me how your career has developed to this point? or

What did you do prior to this role?

This simply provides some background for the interviewer(s) and allows you to settle down into the conversation.

Important point: the introductory few minutes is a useful time to sell yourself and your background. It is a great opportunity to mention anything that is a little obscure in your CV and sell it as a benefit. For example, 'As you can see from my CV twenty years ago I joined a circus for five years. It may seem unconventional but I learnt a lot about running a small business and motivating people during my time there.'

At some point during the interview (and they may start with this one) there will be the inevitable, 'How did you find the assessment centre?'

Do not joke or say anything disparaging – your comments, however amusing, will be taken at face value. Instead answer in any of the following ways:

- 'I thought it was interesting. I enjoy being challenged.'
- 'I have undertaken one of these before and I thought it was a good stretch of my skills.'
- 'I actually enjoy this type of exercise because I learn so much about myself.'
- 'It was fine; I hope there is some good feedback!'
- 'I must be strange; I actually enjoy these activities.'
- 'I found it a challenge, but then it is good to be challenged once in a while.'

... or something similar.

It is not that I am asking you not to be genuine in your comments, only that whatever you say will be judged and at this stage it does not pay to have your comments misinterpreted.

It may sound old fashioned but do expect a question regarding your strengths and any weaknesses. It may not be phrased as such and could instead be presented as, 'If you overheard someone complimenting you, what would they be saying?' or 'If you overheard someone saying something negative about you, what would they be saying?' What we want here is to give an answer that ensures you are genuine but gives a good impression. I would coach someone to reply, 'I would like to think that they would be saying that they found me firm but fair.' Notice that this response is not too saccharine sweet but is reasonable. Another similar response might be, 'That I am a safe pair of hands, and that I deliver on projects' – remember this is hypothetical and actually no one can really know what is said about them!!

Let's get back to the assessment centre at this point. There may well be some questions that verify your results apart from how you found the day so far. How about, 'In the negotiation activity I noticed that you did not participate as much as the others in the group. Can you explain why that was?'

The immediate reaction to this might be to think 'Oh my goodness – they think I did not do enough! I need to get out of this....' and then come up with some dreadful excuse or defence mechanism – but hold your horses. No one is accusing anyone! They just want your explanation and if it is plausible then you will not lose any marks here (in fact make it a good response and you might even gain some!) So no blaming anyone else, getting angry or trying to change the subject. Instead respond with some comment similar to: 'I found that exercise intense and really had to concentrate throughout. Martin had taken the role of the chair and I was showing respect for that position in that I would not barge across any of the heated discussions. I felt that I actually agreed with most of the comments and therefore did not have more to add, but I did interject over the issue of timing because I felt that the figures quoted were not correct.' In other words give a favourable summary of what you DID do and say. The interviewer may then come up with a further qualifying question, 'So have you ever been in the situation where you have spoken out more fully?' to which you can now qualify with, 'Oh yes. If I felt passionately about a situation I would defend it. When I was with [example company]..I [impressive example response]' – this now allows you to put forward more evidence and could recover the situation.

Questions that test against the role – if you are trying for a role that is a promotion for you then it is highly probable that you don't have lots of experience to back up your claims. For example if you are trying for your first management role then you will probably be short of examples of where and how you have managed situations in the past. If that is the case then you will be questioned in a more case scenario way. This means that you will be offered plenty of 'What if' questions to answer such as, 'If you found that your budget was overspent by a member of your team what would you do?' or 'If a member of staff approached to you say that they had seen someone bragging on a social media site that they had attended a sports event when they were off sick, what would you do?' Therefore it pays to ensure that you have thought through some of the basic mechanisms of working with and managing staff. Even if you are very experienced, expect a question such as 'What do you feel is the most challenging aspect of this role?'

Your USP – this stands for unique selling point. It is highly likely that most of the candidates at an assessment centre will have similar backgrounds, qualifications or experience as you will have all been selected for the same job. However each person will have a very different unique selling point and you need to identify yours so that you can use it to differentiate yourself from everyone else. It may be your calm nature, your brilliance with figures, your ability to change a team around, or possibly the fact that you have a history of delivering projects in time and on budget. Quite simply if you were sitting in front of me for an interview I would ask what you felt differentiated you from the other candidates. I would probably phrase it as, 'What special skills or experience do you bring to the role?' or 'What do we get if we recruit you into this role and not one of the other candidates?' It may sound a direct question but I am asking it for two reasons. I not only want to know what 'extra' the organisation would be gaining if we selected you, but also whether you are self- aware – that is aware and proud of your own unique properties. Self aware people know what their strengths and they use them to add weight to their position. (Conversely they also know their weaknesses and make sure there is ample provision in place to provide protection, thus reducing their negative power).

Therefore before attending the interview, think through:

1.   The whole job, all of the aspects, do you match or not?

2.   If there is a shortfall, what can you say to bolster this area up and convince the interviewers to take a chance?

3.   If there are still areas where you feel insecure, how are you going to present these as development areas to the interviewer?

4.   Be honest with yourself, were there aspects of your performance in the activities that may cause comment? – if so, have a response ready.

5.   What do you think are your main strengths and weaknesses?

6. What is your USP?

7. The main points YOU wish to find out and get across during the interview

There will always be a section at the end where you will be asked whether you have any further questions. Try to have one because again, it will demonstrate that you appear to have thought through the job and want to know more. Also having questions shows keenness and engagement.

Exercise: read through the case study for BabyMaxPro again and write a list on the following page of questions you would ask if you were interviewing for the post of a general manager.

Well there are many questions you could have asked including:

Can you tell me a little about your background?

What skills and abilities lead you to believe that you would fit into BabyMaxPro?

What do you know about the company?

Tell us about your experience in management?

Have you ever worked with the pharmaceutical industry before?

What challenges do you see?

What is your opinion regarding the way that the structure in BabyMaxPro is organised?

Just looking at the information you have received, if you could make one immediate change in BabyMaxPro what would it be?

Where do you think BabyMaxPro's future lies?

What do you personally bring to the role and how will that help us achieve our vision?

How would you take forward our Principles?

What is your opinion of our survey results?

Given the results of our survey what action would you, as general manager, take?

Practice answering each question – what would you say?

HOW SHOULD YOU ACT?

In a nutshell, professionally

Usually the interview comes on the same day as the assessment centre and is part of it, and therefore you should still be in your smart clothes. You will have been on show all day and performing to your best ability and it would be understandable if you felt that you could now start to relax a little – but don't fall into that trap. You need to stay keen and ready to take on every question in a professional manner.

When you enter the room, go forward and shake hands with the interviewer or panel (especially if this is a management role). It will make you appear forthright and if you are moving into a management or professional role, you would be expected to be able to introduce yourself to guests and be confident enough to step forward. Shake hands with a firm, strong (but not knuckle breaking) gesture. If you are at all unsure, practice on a colleague or mate before going. Believe it or not a limp handshake can lose you the position even if your answers are respectable.

If there is a chair for you, sit in it and make yourself comfortable, with your hands in your lap or on your legs (not crossed in front of your chest or hanging by your sides). If you need your hands to hold something it is absolutely fine to take notes into an interview but make sure they are in a smart book or folder, and leave your phone on silent mode.

Eye contact is crucial. Look at the interviewer or along the panel making sure you make eye contact with each person there – it will break down so many barriers before you begin to speak. As each person speaks to you, make sure that you answer by making eye contact at the same time as responding. It is fine to sweep your gaze across the whole line of the panel as long as you return back to the person asking the question and give them the majority of your attention.

Try to keep anxiety gestures (touching around the facial area, playing with a pen or jewellery, fiddling with earrings or hair) to a minimum as they actually make you look more nervous. You cannot always avoid verbal anxieties such as stuttering, ummming and errring but unless extreme these are much less noticeable than you think.

At the end of your interview, thank the panel or interviewer and offer a handshake again before turning and moving smartly back through the door.

In summary:

1. The interview is a chance to get your message across and push home any additional skills.

2. The interviewer or panel will be looking to confirm or change their mind about your assessment so far.

3. The interviewers will want to know what makes you stand out from other candidates – so make sure you have thought about this and know how to promote your USP.

4. Interviews are typically 15–90 minutes long. See this as an opportunity to shine through.

5. Check out that you have a good handshake and use it.

6. Don't be afraid to offer up more experience and information if you believe a point is important.

7. Act, dress and be the person they want in the job. Live it as if it were real and you will convince everyone that you are the right person for the job.

CHAPTER 9
FEEDBACK

I discussed feedback briefly in Chapter 3 but here I want to pick up the subject in a little more detail.

Feedback is one of those strange things that is great when it is good and very difficult to take when it is not so complimentary.

Important point: in this context all feedback is given in response to the job you have applied for, within that organisational setting, and based on your observed performance. This is not a cop out or to be used as an easy excuse if you don't like what you hear: if your performance was poor then you need to consider why and what you want to do about that. However, let's just look at those three points in more detail:

The job – if you have applied for a job that is a real stretch, and perhaps you do not have the experience or history to back it up, then of course you are going to have to explain how you intend making up for that shortfall – and no matter how much you feel you can make up this shortfall in your skills/knowledge/ability/experience, your assessor/interviewer may thing differently. For example, if you are applying for your first senior management position in a large organisation and until now you have held a middle management position in a small organisation, you might be perceived as a bit of a risk. After all, management and supervisory titles are notoriously misleading, for example a supervisor in a large company could have far more responsibility, authority and budget than a general manager of a small company. This is why the content and tasks of your current and previous positions will need to be assessed. You do not have to be an exact fit for the new role but any manager employing you needs to know where there are development needs and whether the organisation is prepared to develop you in these areas. Therefore the feedback you will receive following an assessment centre will be based on the job you are applying for; it will be context specific, and you need to view it through this lens.

The organisation – the feedback will also be based on you working in that specific organisation. I once applied for a consultancy job within a company that I really did not consider enough in detail. I reasoned that it was the job I wanted, I felt I could do it well, and knew that as I would be working out in the field with other companies most of the time, I would be on the road a lot of the time. I foolishly did not consider the values of the company I was applying to – my focus was out with my customers and not with my colleagues. I had failed to consider that the contracts I would be working on had been won through the values of the company itself, and worse, when I actually looked at their values, they were not totally in alignment with my own business values at that time (I was more in tune with the private sector and they were aimed at the voluntary and health sector). I was not offered the job and the feedback I received showed that I was not right for their organisation – and rightly so, although I found that difficult to accept at the time! I was focussing on the job and they were focussing on me as an employee in the organisation, and the two are not always the same.

Your observed performance – we all mess up sometimes, no matter how polished our rehearsals may be. You only have to watch any of the celebrity 'skill-type' TV programmes to know that hours in preparation can only take you so far, there is still the 'performance' to get through; and sometimes it just goes wrong on the day. Some of this may be acceptable to the assessors (depending on your performance in the other activities) but it may be something that they cannot overlook. You need to be honest with yourself – was it a mistake or could you have planned things better? If it really was just nerves it is disappointing, but there are occasions when sometimes fate steps in, and you have to rationalise that, for whatever reason, this job was somehow not for you.

HOW TO DEAL WITH FEEDBACK

There are two aspects here, dealing with it outwardly and inwardly. The first is the face we show to the world and the second is how we feel inside – and they may be very different.

Receiving great feedback is not too difficult and therefore I am going to concentrate on receiving difficult feedback here. Let's first of all start on the outside.

The amount of preparation you have for this may be limited. It may be what you expect or it may be a complete surprise – perhaps you thought you did great, and someone now is telling you a different story. This may be compounded by the fact that in some cases the feedback will be given face to face and in others, over the phone or even by electronic means (email or text). The important aspect of accepting face to face negative comments is to detach. The comments are not levelled at you as a person, they are observed behaviour, and therefore no one is saying that you are a bad person, just that you did not perform well in that particular activity. In many cases the person giving you feedback may have a point and if so, then acknowledge that with a nod or "I see." However, if they are more tentative in their suggestions, such as saying, "We observed that in this activity you did not demonstrate an opinion, is that so?" then they are inviting you to explain or justify why you acted as you did. If this is the case then there is an opportunity for you to redeem your actions, and you may yet make it to the next round. I have had many applicants explain their actions and still go on to secure roles within the company, based on the way they handled their feedback.

Face to face: if you are going to meet someone for feedback, expect that there should be a balance between what you did well and what was not so good. They will be looking at you and trying to judge from your face, how you feel about the situation. However, be aware that your reaction to their words may or may not change the message. What I mean here is that just because you find their comments hurtful, does not mean that they will hold back, and therefore it is no use feigning vulnerability in the hope that the person giving you feedback will feel sorry for you and choose to flatter you instead. Far better instead to treat it professionally. Take a pen and paper pad with you to make notes and look as though you are listening, asking questions if necessary. Use paraphrasing to ensure you get the correct message and clarify any misunderstandings, "So you are saying that my main areas for losing points were in my indecisiveness, is that correct?"

At the end of the feedback session ask any final questions and thank the person for their time. Although feedback is best practice it is not a legal requirement and therefore it shows a commitment by the other person or organisation towards trying to help the delegates understand the outcome of the assessment centre and develop further if necessary. Many people take on board the feedback, make the adjustments or undertake additional learning and go on to secure future jobs with that organisation! It is something I have done myself and helped many others to achieve – and therefore it is well worth listening.

Feedback on the phone: this is somewhat different in that there is no face or body language for either of you. Even so, try to take the call when you are in private and unlikely to get distractions, such as someone bursting in. As before, keep a pen and paper by the telephone and note down any points. Don't forget to say "Yes" and "Ah" or "Ummm" occasionally to help the caller know that you are there, and end the call by clarifying any actions (if necessary), paraphrasing a summary of the call, and then thanking them for their time. The impression you wish to give is one of having listened intently and been interested in what they have to say. It is absolutely fine to ask questions (including whether there is likely to be another similar position coming up in the future) it shows keenness and interest.

Electronic feedback: this is rare but still happens. The reason for its rarity is that it is unusual to find anyone who will put feedback in writing, in case of legal challenge. I think in this instance you also need to consider whether you actually want to work for a company that delivers sensitive information in this way.

Now let's think about what is going on inside. The likelihood is that you will be feeling very nervous and anxious. What will they say? Will it be mainly good? Did I do most things right or was I a complete wash out? The danger is that their words will be overshadowed by your own emotions and then you will not absorb anything, and further, you will feel a complete failure. It is not often we actively ask anyone to criticise us and so it is not surprising that we feel challenged and hurt by the comments of others. Here are some tips to help you remain sane, and be able to bounce back:

1. Listen to what is said and write down the EXACT words. It is very easy to confuse what was actually said after the event, and paint over your own interpretation.

2. Take deep breaths – this is only a job and there will always be another. You may be disappointed but no one has actually died here.

3. Be totally honest, was their observation justifiable? For example if you said nothing during the team exercise, you cannot blame them for commenting on that, no matter that you felt that you could not get a word in sideways.

4. Try to see how they came to their conclusions. In the example above, if you do not speak during a meeting it could be perceived by an onlooker that you had nothing to contribute. By rationalising what happened we can try to accept the results even if we don't like them.

5. Consider how you would undertake this exercise if you were called to do it again and make some notes of your thoughts. What would you do differently? (Don't just write down that you would speak up next time, how would you interject so that it did not just look like you were shouting the other person down? How would you manage to get your point across – and what actually would be your point?)

6. Think about how their comments fit into any other feedback you have had. If there is a pattern or repeated message here, perhaps it is time to start listening and recognising that this behaviour is actually what you are exhibiting, and possibly needs to change.

7. Make a commitment to change or develop, and get some support. If you feel that the feedback is justifiable and you really want a job like this, then only personal change or advancement will get you to where you want to be. How do you do that? Well read on...

PUTTING FEEDBACK INTO ACTION

The essential point with feedback is that you do something with it, otherwise it is just words. If you really want that top job and you keep being told that you don't have the skills, what do you do?

Firstly try to identify specifically what the problem is. 'I don't make the grade' is vague and unhelpful. 'I don't make myself heard in meetings' or 'I need to be a sharper negotiator' is more specific and can be worked on.

If you currently work in a place where you have appraisals or development sessions with your manager, then speak to them about this. (You do not have to mention that you have been for another job if you would rather not. Just say that this is an area you would like to develop as part of your ongoing personal development). If you do not have appraisals or work in an environment where personal development is on the agenda, then you will need to work on these issues by yourself (or with a colleague). You could try:

Modelling – identify someone whom you admire and try to 'people-watch' their style. How do they command attention? Call a room to order? Cut through the chatter? Negotiate? You can learn so much from watching others who have learnt before you.

Secondments – secondments are when you are able to undertake a different job whilst your current post is held open for you. It is a form of development where you can essentially try out a position before deciding that this is what you want.

Observations – this used to be called 'sitting by Nellie' and really means learning a job whilst sitting by the most proficient member of staff to watch them. These days you can request to sit and observe someone for half a day or a full day and it can be a great way of learning a particular topic such as budget management. This technique also blends into workshadowing where you are literally following around another member of staff to see what they do. This is a great way to gain a slice of life for a senior manager or Chief Executive before deciding whether it is really for you.

Standing in – offer to stand in for your manager at every opportunity, covering their meetings and undertaking presentations. Quite simply the more you do this the more comfortable you will feel in that position, and this will come over as both confidence and experience at your next assessment centre.

Have a makeover – sometimes it is refreshing to change. If the feedback was about your personal presentation, be honest about your clothes and hair. Invest is a couple of key items and start to dress for the position you want, rather than where you are now.

Top up your knowledge – read the broadsheets and professional websites. Even if the job you wanted is in a niche area you will be expected to be up to date with current affairs and have an opinion. Also read management books to further your knowledge around the theories of subjects, and any 'how to' book such as this one, is great for tackling specific issues. If you get the opportunity, also attend conferences. You can network in addition to increasing your knowledge. If cost is an issue, visit your local library where there are many resources to help you.

Attend training – if you are able to request specific training then do so, or if you are not able to do that, consider making a personal investment. Also make the most of your training. Enter into it knowing exactly what you want out of the session, and make sure you achieve it. Then ensure you put it into practice. Training should not be a spectator sport, you need to be fully involved to get the most from it.

Coaching – if you feel that you need one-to-one attention to help you focus on specific issues that need a change of behaviour, then consider working with a coach. Although initially this may seem expensive it can work out cheaper in the long run as you can achieve much in a lunchtime session, leaving the rest of your day free to generate more business.

Whatever method you choose, there is a new career opportunity out there waiting for you. So many times I have heard initial disappointment change into, "Well actually it was a good job I did not get that job because just afterwards something better turned up," or some similar comment. There are some great jobs out there, but only for those who go for it. If you are moving up in the world of work, there will be yet another assessment centre to go through, and so working on your skills now will pay dividends in the future. As Thomas Jefferson once said, "I am a great believer in luck and I find that the harder I work, the more I have of it."

BABYMAXPRO
CASE STUDY FOR YOUR ASSESSMENT CENTRE

INTRODUCTION

The purpose of the exercises you are being asked to complete will give you the opportunity to show how you apply your skills against work-based competencies. The case study ensures that every candidate has the same amount of information regarding the company and will provide you with all the background information you need.

BACKGROUND

You are an employee wanting to secure a general management job at BabyMaxPro. On the following pages you will find a background to the company (such as you would find in a business plan or corporate document) and some additional information in the form of reports and emails.

YOUR TASK

The information presented here will form the background to the various exercises in the assessment centre and will be referred to throughout this book. Read them thoroughly and make notes regarding any aspect you find interesting or where you feel you can impact on this company.

The information given here is completely fictitious and is not based on any real organisation. The information is simulated and therefore you will need to use your own judgement, knowledge and experience to look through the documentation and draw conclusions.

Please note: You do not need any specialist industry knowledge to undertake this task. This example is to be used only with this book. When experiencing a real assessment centre, you will be provided with an example more suited to the industry you are joining or applicable to the role.

ABOUT BABYMAXPRO

BabyMaxPro formed in 1996 when Pharmacists Helen Maxwell and Shaun Maxwell wanted to produce the highest factor skin block for babies on the market. Their son, Callum was born in 1995 with hyper-sensitive skin and they found that none of the proprietary sun blocks on the market at that time both suited his skin and provided the protection he needed. The name comes from the words 'baby maximum protection' as that is what Helen and Shaun were seeking.

The first creams and lotions were created from their kitchen, but after being featured in a national newspaper, they soon realised that they needed additional premises. BabyMaxPro cream remains a high selling cream with sales of over 2.5 million units around the world, netting the company just under £7 Million per annum. Today the cream is manufactured by Lincoln Pharmaceuticals under contract and the formula remains top secret.

Following the initial success of BabyMaxPro cream, Helen and Shaun developed their baby range to include moisturiser and bath products. These products complement the range and although they are gentle for a baby's skin, they do not contain any specific 'secret' formula. In 1998 Lincoln Pharmaceuticals could not take on this additional range due to their size and the anticipated demand and therefore the bath range is produced by Helix Laboratories. The baby range, although highly profitable, did not achieve the same demand as the original BabyMaxPro cream, and the contract for Helix is up for re-consideration in the next 12 months.

In 2000 Helen Maxwell was asked to judge a competition to find the best female entrepreneur. Although the winner of the competition was Linda Clarke with her 'In a Box' design your own wedding kit, Helen was impressed by another entrant, Kimberly Cresswell who had designed a new feeding cup. Helen felt the feeder cup fitted BabyMaxPro and so she offered Kimberly a deal on working together with BabyMaxPro to launch the product under the BabyMaxPro label. Kimberly jumped at the chance and this section of the business now produces all feeding ware including plastic bibs. These are sold under the banner of BabyMaxPro Essentials.

In 2002 at a similar event Helen met fellow judge Paul Dickinson who told her about a new and very different educational toy for very young children that he had designed. Helen made the same offer and the toy, together with five other educational toys now make up the BabyMaxPro Learning range.

In 2004 the company hit a setback when they tried to launch a clothing line, BabyMaxPro Design. The clothes although beautifully made with natural fabrics were too expensive for the market and could not stand up against cheap imports. It folded after a year, losing the company £3 million in investments, but the two employees on the team were able to be absorbed into the BabyMaxPro Cream and Baby Care team and there were no redundancies. It is very little discussed as it caused many real problems within the company.

Since 2004 the company has not invested in any new areas even though they recognise that there has been significant cultural changes in that space of time. Although BabyMaxPro is financially safe the owners are feeling that it is losing its entrepreneurial image and is in danger of becoming staid and out of touch. BabyMaxPro also has a charitable arm and gives 5% of its profits to infant mortality projects in third world countries.

The ethos of BabyMaxpro has never been to make huge profits. Helen and Shaun care more about providing employment for local people and helping the economy through sustaining jobs. They also want to help other entrepreneurs to find a foothold in the market by offering them an outlet for their inventions through the BabyProMax company.

INSIDE BABYMAXPRO

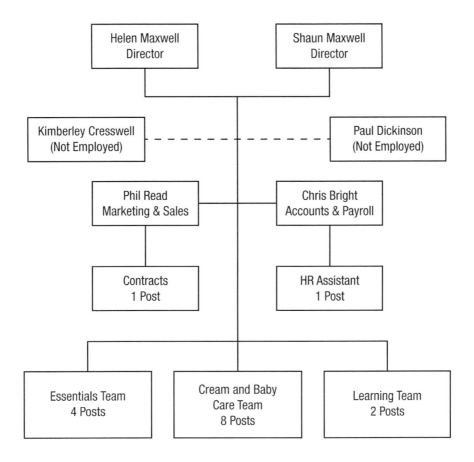

Helen Maxwell
Director

Shaun Maxwell
Director

Kimberley Cresswell
(Not Employed)

Paul Dickinson
(Not Employed)

Phil Read
Marketing & Sales

Chris Bright
Accounts & Payroll

Contracts
1 Post

HR Assistant
1 Post

Essentials Team
4 Posts

Cream and Baby
Care Team
8 Posts

Learning Team
2 Posts

HOW WE WORK
IN BABYPROMAX

At BabyProMax we value certain behaviours and work to a set of principles that we believe create a favourable working atmosphere, company growth and sustainability.

Our Principles:

Focus on the Customer

Commercial Awareness

Respect for Everyone

Collaboration

Innovation

The BabyMaxPro Principles

COMMERCIAL AWARENESS

We understand that it is important to compete financially and maintain the commercial health of the business. Without sales and our commercial footing BabyProMax would not exist. To secure a prosperous future we need to ensure that every employee is business aware and that we are able to deliver a healthy return on investment.

COLLABORATION

BabyProMax has drawn great strength in working in collaboration with other organisations and entrepreneurs. We also have a history of delivering through great team work. We know that we need to share our capabilities and work together to provide a collective brilliance to compete in the market for tomorrow.

INNOVATION

BabyProMax is born out of innovation and is known and respected for its creativity. We embrace change and help to nurture new ideas. We actively seek out new ideas from every area of the business, and we are not afraid to invest time in nurturing new talent.

RESPECT FOR EVERYONE

We wish to create an environment where every member of BabyMaxPro feels heard and valued. All staff deserve to work in an environment free from harassment and intimidation; where difference is not only valued but celebrated for the richness it brings to the future of the business.

FOCUS ON THE CUSTOMER

BabyMaxPro does not exist without customers, and many customers have been loyal to the company since its inception. We aim to honour that loyalty to both our original and new customers by always putting them at the forefront of any business decisions.

THE BABYMAXPRO VISION FOR THE FUTURE

Due to steady sales of BabyMaxPro cream we have been fortunate to retain a stronghold in the sun protection area of our business. However, we now need to reduce that risk by strengthening our other brands whilst at the same time, searching for solid innovation.

From this year all areas of the business will have their own business plans that demonstrate individual growth and sustainability. We will still continue to nurture new ideas and concepts but within an ordered timeframe.

In the coming year, we also need to recapture the essence that made BabyProMax an original, innovative company. Therefore we will be looking to expand into at least one new area of business that both complements and grows the BabyMaxPro brand.

OVERVIEW OF THE ANNUAL COLLEAGUE SURVEY

There was 100% response rate to this very popular staff feedback tool.

This year's key findings	Yes	No	Last year's results for comparison	Yes	No
I have confidence in the direction of the company	99%	1%	I have confidence in the direction of the company	100%	0%
I am happy in my job	33%	77%	I am happy in my job	65%	35%
I feel involved and listened to	27%	73%	I feel involved and listened to	48%	52%
My ideas are discussed in full with the team or my manager	21%	79%	My ideas are discussed in full with the team or my manager	57%	43%
I understand my role fully	75%	25%	I understand my role fully	57%	43%
I am bored in my role	50%	50%	I am bored in my role	20%	80%
I have good opportunities to develop	20%	80%	I have good opportunities to develop	20%	80%
I receive leadership from my line manager	40%	60%	I receive leadership from my line manager	45%	55%
I am proud to be a part of BabyMaxPro	98%	2%	I am proud to be a part of BabyMaxPro	97%	3%
I believe there is a future in BabyMaxPro	100%	0%	I believe there is a future in BabyMaxPro	100%	0%

EMAIL

Hi

I have just come back from a new (possible) client, and I am so excited I want to report back. Gareth and Stacy Johns live in Wales and started out making recyclable baby pants from their own sheep's wool. The baby pants are high in lanolin which soothes baby's skin and creates a waterproof barrier that reduces leaks. The pants hold a nappy liner, which is easily disposed, thus cutting down on waste. They have been selling to their dedicated customers for a couple of years with great success and they are creating quite a following, although they are a very small enterprise, possibly only selling in the region of 100 – 150 units per year.

As the farm has been caught in the farming recession they have invested in a new range of babies clothing, again based on the wool from their flock of 'baby faced doll' sheep. The range is very simple: vests, socks, simple cardigans and tights, mainly in cream. The clothing is organic and has been spun in a way that ensures it is exceptionally soft. They are aiming their product at those parents who have an interest in supporting small companies and wish to help the environment.

Gareth and Stacey believe that if they are to take this brand to the next level, they need the backing and support of a larger enterprise. What are your thoughts? Can someone look at this?

Phil Read

EMAIL

Hi

I am sending this from an exhibition at the NEC.

I have just met with a company called MeandMama who make buggies and car seats. Briefly, their design is fairly standard but their safety features and quality is second to none. In a nutshell, they cannot exist much longer in the current marketplace on their own and they are looking for a company to partner with (or even for a buyout) – someone bigger, with established customers. When I told them that BabyMaxPro may be interested they were thrilled and felt that this was just the kind of business they would want to associate their products with. I don't know whether we are interested at all but I am going to ask them to come down to us in about a month to have a conversation as to whether we might be of mutual assistance.

I also wanted to tell you that I have seen a product BabySunSafe that is very similar to BabyMaxPro cream and is selling at half our price.

Chris Bright

(Sent from my phone)

EMAIL

Hi

I have been speaking with a number of providers in respect of introducing a leadership programme into the company. Although I have searched the net widely there does not seem to be anyone out there offering exactly what we want for our employees. I think therefore we should be thinking along the lines of commissioning a bespoke programme that fits our principles.

Can you work up some ideas (and possibly some costs) for me to take to the board as soon as possible?

Many thanks

Mary Stevens

(HR Assistant)